I've spent over 30 years in sales – as an individ [barcode: I0069906] manager, VP, industry executive, CRO, and Presider is a true playbook for success at every level of an organization.

In full transparency, I was a client of Simon's about ten years ago, and he remains one of the best executive trainers and coaches I've worked with. There are coaches who've never played the game, and then there are those – like Simon – who were top performers and chose to become force multipliers by selflessly teaching others.

Stop Managing Start Leading exemplifies this mindset. It's practical, insightful, and deeply impactful. This will be my go-to book gift for my team and colleagues in 2025. Brilliant work!

Brad Copeland,
President, FileBank Inc.

As the Founder of a Global Sales Transformation Company, I was lucky enough to work with Simon with multiple global clients. Never has it been truer that the differentiator for any company is how its top people show up in front of clients. Simon is a master consultant and one of the best presenters and keynote speakers I have had the privilege to work with. His book is a testament to taking his insights and having the credibility and presence to be able to deliver those live to clients with amazing results.

Chris Norton,
CRO Positive Intelligence, Inc.,
Founder and author of *The DNA of Success*

Stop Managing Start Leading is a breakthrough book in sales leadership – practical, inspiring, and long overdue. It's for sales managers, CEOs, and reps ready to trade control for coaching, pressure for purpose. Backed by real data and stories, Simon shows how true leadership – not management – is the key to high-growth sales teams.

Aaron Norris,
Executive Sales Coach and author of *Sales Life*

After years of leading teams, I thought I'd seen every leadership strategy – but Simon Jackson still managed to surprise me. He shines a spotlight on how my own mindset might be the toughest barrier to success. By focusing on personal accountability and growth, Jackson offers a blueprint that resonates even with veteran executives. It's an engaging reminder that to truly lead others, we must first learn to lead ourselves.

Jamie Anderson,
President, UserTesting

Having known Simon for several years, I have seen the impact of his thinking firsthand. His ability to distil the complexity of sales leadership into actionable, values-led ideas is rare, and *Stop Managing Start Leading* is a brilliant example. Simon reminds us that the real differentiator is leadership rooted in values, clarity, and coaching. This isn't a theoretical manual, it's a field-tested guide built on years of insight and grounded in lived experience. Anyone serious about building a high-performance, people-first sales culture should read this. It's an important addition to the leadership bookshelf.

Matt Webb,
CEO, Mentor Group and author of *Infinite Selling*

This is a practical and inspiring guide that echoes much of what I've championed through *SUMO* – mindset, resilience, and real conversations. One line that stood out for me: 'It's not through changing your team that you'll achieve success, but by changing yourself.' A message more leaders need to hear. If you lead a sales team – or aspire to – you'll find plenty in here to reflect on and apply.

Paul McGee,
The SUMO Guy; international speaker,
Sunday Times best-selling author

Simon Jackson's *Stop Managing, Start Leading* truly captures what it takes to lead modern sales teams – with the kind of clarity, empathy, and insight I value. This book equips leaders with the tools to 'get on the same frequency' as their people: listening deeply, empowering through coaching, and building a secure, performance-focused culture. Having witnessed Simon's coaching in action, I can confidently say this book will help take any sales leader to the next level.

Brian McCarthy,
CRO, Rubrik

I've known Simon for many years, and I respect the depth of experience he brings, as both a successful sales leader and a skilled coach. This book is full of the kind of wisdom that only comes from doing the job, day in and day out, with real teams and real targets. Simon knows and understands the pressures sales leaders face and offers practical ways to make coaching a genuine part of the job, not just an added extra.

Simon hasn't overwhelmed the reader with a long list of coaching tools or complex leadership models either. Instead, he's carefully curated a small number of practical, focused exercises and frameworks that are genuinely useful – and specifically designed with the realities of sales leadership in mind. Simon's belief in developing people in organizations runs through every page. This is a realistic, encouraging and much-needed guide for anyone who wants to lead well and help their team thrive.

Kim Morgan,
MA, MCC, Founder and Chairperson
of Barefoot Coaching Ltd

This book flips the outdated idea that salespeople need managing. They don't – and as Simon shows, what they need is leadership. Through clear frameworks and thoughtful guidance, he shows how high standards and great performance come not from control, but from purpose, clarity, and learning. He doesn't shy away from the challenges leaders face when pulled in different – and often conflicting – directions. Instead, he provides a practical roadmap for navigating them. The result? A more fulfilling environment where people thrive and success is sustainable. For anyone serious about leading in sales, this is essential reading.

Andrew Hough,
Founder and Director, Institute of Sales Professionals

STOP MANAGING
START LEADING

Unlocking the **secrets** *to building a high-growth sales team*

Simon Jackson

First published in Great Britain by Practical Inspiration Publishing, 2025

ISBN   978-1-78860-845-9 (paperback)
        978-1-78860-844-2 (hardback)
        978-1-78860-846-6 (ebook)

EU GPSR representative: LOGOS EUROPE, 9 rue Nicolas Poussin, LA ROCHELLE 17000, France Contact@logoseurope.eu

Want to bulk-buy copies of this book for your team and colleagues? We can customize the content and co-brand *Stop Managing Start Leading* to suit your business's needs.

Please email info@practicalinspiration.com for more details.

Practical Inspiration
Publishing

To Grace, Daisy, and Eden
You are my greatest joy, my inspiration, my purpose

Contents

Foreword

There is a fabulous concept in psychology called *the illusion of explanatory depth* which describes our belief that we understand more about the world than we actually do.

It is often not until we are asked to actually explain a concept, that we come face to face with our limited understanding of it.

Think of those people who rail against the inadequacies of our political systems without understanding how to fix it, or those who watch elite sport and diagnose the glaring errors they assume those playing it have missed. In my own case, I bump up against this concept whenever I am faced with DIY tasks: 'I have no idea what I am doing.'

If you are a sales leader, this book is the antidote.

Let Simon take you into the details of what it takes to build a high-growth sales team with his customary style and flair for making the complex simple, the direction clear, and the actions obvious.

His coaching work, honed over many years in the world of helping to shape successful sales teams, is exceptional. This work shows his writing to be equally impressive.

I am confident you will enjoy reading this book, time and time again.

Professor Damian Hughes,
Sunday Times best-selling author and performance coach

Introduction

'Have you ever considered that the problem might be you?' And then the silence. That awkward silence.

I was sat across from Robert and we were just 20 minutes into our very first meeting. There was a large boardroom-style table separating us and proudly displayed all around were samples of the products that Robert and his teams were charged to sell. Robert broke eye contact first. I could tell he didn't like my question. The fact is, it was more of a statement than a question, and it had to be said.

We had been introduced by a mutual friend who thought that there could be value in us talking. Robert was the VP of Sales for a large manufacturing company. He has been with the company for several years and was a respected member of the leadership team. But he had started to come under intense pressure to improve his sales performance. The company had been growing, but despite multiple initiatives and investments it was being outpaced by its competitors.

For the last 20 minutes Robert had been describing all the challenges he was facing. As far as he was concerned it all boiled down to one issue. As he put it, 'we just can't seem to hire the right people.' He talked me through his approach and how he had invested heavily in recruiting experienced salespeople from within his industry who'd demonstrated outstanding performance, luring them away from his competitors with offers of high salaries and juicy incentives. But once they were in, his expectations were often disappointed; even with all that experience, they still didn't perform. Some of them would leave of their own accord within a few months, and others would hang around for a while longer but would be managed out of the business before the end of their first year.

'I just can't understand what their problem is,' Robert had said.

I let the silence do its magic.

❈

Sales is the lifeblood of any business. What company could survive if it didn't sell anything? How would it grow if it didn't increase its turnover? When you work in sales, you're at the forefront of making your organization a success. This is one of the reasons I personally love sales.

That's the good side, but I know from experience there's more to it than that. Especially when it comes to being the *manager* of a sales team rather than an individual contributor. You still have targets and quotas to meet, but now you have to motivate other people to achieve them; that might be easy with some of your team members, but with others it can be a headache. There are always deals that will fall through if you don't step in, or people who aren't proactive enough to keep your pipeline topped up without you constantly being on their case.

One of the extra burdens of management is the creation of endless reports and plans. Sometimes it feels as if all you do is hold meetings, write forecasts, and firefight the latest problem to raise its head. On a bad day it can be tempting to gaze back wistfully into the past, when all you had to worry about was your own sales record. Are you now a glorified administrator, issuing orders and writing reports? Surely there's a bigger reason for your role than that. And if so, what? It's moments like these when being a sales manager can seem like the loneliest, most frustrating job in the world.

Of course, you might not be as overwhelmed as I've assumed. Maybe you've picked up this book because you feel that you're doing okay but have a sneaking suspicion that you could be better. Either way, there's a gap between where you are now and where you want to be. The problem is, you're not sure what that gap consists of and how to bridge it.

This book answers those questions. I'm here to tell you that the solution to your problems lies within you. In other words, it's not through changing your team that you'll achieve success, but by changing yourself. The turning point will come when you transition from being a sales manager to a sales leader. This means developing your team. Because when your role is to achieve difficult things through other people, improving how those people work becomes your primary goal.

It's a lesson that I learned through my own sales career. I've worked in sales and leadership development for over 30 years, first as an individual salesperson and later as a sales manager and leader in some of the UK's largest companies. These days, I'm a consultant, trainer, and mentor for people in organizations all over the world who want to develop their sales leadership capabilities. I love helping them to grow as leaders so that they can inspire their teams. I seek to learn from great leaders, and I lean on research in neuroscience and social psychology to understand what makes them tick.

The reason I've written this book is because it's the one I wish I'd had when I was promoted to a sales management position all those years ago. Then, I didn't understand that developing my team was the key to unlocking sales success, and even if I had, I wouldn't have known how to go about it. It was only after many years of training and personal development of my own that I saw the light. How many wasted hours and lost opportunities could I have saved, if I'd known then what I know now? How many more deals could my team have won? How much better could the people in my team have been if only I had helped them realize their true potential. It's frustrating to think about, but rather than dwell on it I've turned my attention to helping others so they can shortcut the learning curve that I went through.

In Part 1 of the book, we start with you, the sales manager (or rather, the sales leader-in-waiting). Here we explore the root causes of sales performance issues, and how you can start to address them. In Part 2, we build your leadership skills so that you feel confident enough to step up to the leadership challenge ahead. And in Part 3 we get practical; here you'll learn numerous ways of motivating, inspiring, and organizing your team. By the end, you'll feel like a true sales leader in the making.

One thing before we move forward: there's a world of difference between knowing something and doing it. In fact, I'd even go so far as to say that you know much of what's in this book already. But are you doing it? And if not, why is that? Is it because you don't believe it's right? If so, that's fine, as long as you've tried it and have evidence that it doesn't work. But what if you don't have that evidence? What if you've never attempted it wholeheartedly, assuming that it's not for you or that there's no point? This is when it's time to take a fresh look and be open minded about trying something different.

There may be moments during the following chapters when you feel a little uncomfortable. Please don't dismiss those feelings, but take note of them and consider why they're there. It might be because there's an inconsistency between what you know to do and what you're actually doing, in which case you already have the remedy: just give my suggestions a go. You could be pleasantly surprised at the results.

Let's start by taking a look at your role and the issues you face. We're ready to begin Part 1.

PART 1

YOU

Being a sales manager can feel like an impossible job at times. However, it's not because it can't be rewarding and enjoyable, but because you've probably come to the wrong conclusions about what's causing the pain. When you know the source, you can apply the remedy. In this part of the book, you'll learn where to look for solutions, and how to develop your confidence when becoming a leader.

Chapter 1
The real problem

I'd like to take you back to a day which probably doesn't mean much to you, but that's engraved on my memory forever. The date was Monday 15 September, 2008, and was the day Lehman Brothers filed for Chapter 11 bankruptcy protection. It was also the day that marked the start of one of the worst financial crises in history.

Why did it matter to me personally? Because at the time I was Corporate Sector Sales Head at Vodafone. As I heard the news on the radio, my first thought was: 'Do they owe us any money?' And then, more seriously: 'Who's going to be next?' It was obvious to me that a company such as Vodafone, which held a significant market share across all industry sectors, was going to be massively affected by the event; the fact that we'd been growing successfully for many years was not going to insulate us against the downturn to come. I wasn't wrong. By the end of that financial year our service revenues were in decline for the first time ever.

This prompted senior leaders to ask questions about our sales teams. 'Were they just lucky before, riding on the winds of market growth? And are they good enough to step up to this new challenge today?' I spent the next few months staggering from one stressful meeting to the next, either with those who offloaded their problems from above, or with my teams who were asking for assurance and motivation from below. In the snatched moments between meetings, I'd sit at my laptop with my stomach churning, trying to think my way through the mess.

However, the global financial crisis wasn't the only challenge that Sales was facing. Like many organizations, we were in the middle of a perfect storm in which various external factors were transforming the way we competed in our marketplace and operated internally. For us, we also had two of our major competitors merging to form a company much larger than ours, which meant we had to extend our portfolio into new areas. I'm sure you can think of similar issues that are facing your own business. Can you recognize any of the ones below?

We're living in a VUCA world

Think about what we've been dealing with since the start of the 21st century: the 2008 global economic crisis, political upheavals such as Brexit, the COVID-19 pandemic, and the Great Resignation. As I write this, there is war in mainland Europe. No doubt these are challenging times. We are facing unprecedented inflation in a recessive market compounded by labour and supply issues that adds increasing difficulty to our ability to grow.[1]

This is what's often referred to as a 'VUCA world' – a Volatile, Uncertain, Complex, and Ambiguous situation that's taken our old certainties and thrown them up in the air. It's the environment that all organizations operate within today. What were once-in-a-lifetime challenges are occurring more regularly.

And yet to a certain extent this is nothing new. In fact, many of these issues are eerily familiar. If you look back 100 years, there was world war, economic depression, and a global flu pandemic. It's just that we humans are so resistant to change that anything that rocks our world feels hard to deal with, whether it's 'new' or not. Uncertainty and instability impact us on both an individual and an organizational level, affecting how we operate and what we do. Sales leaders are constantly asking themselves: 'How can I structure my team to cope with this ever-changing environment? Should we be leaner, flatter, or what? How can we be more agile?' This places a demand on everyone's mental and emotional resources, leaving less energy for anything else.

The nature of the sales role has changed

Gone are the days when the salesperson was the fount of all knowledge. People are doing their own research[2] and can now learn about what you sell online, so they're more empowered than ever before. There's research showing that a potential customer in a business-to-business environment can be up to 57% of the way through their buying process before they even engage with an organization at a personal level,[3] and that salespeople have only 5% of a customer's time during their buying journey.[4] The question to ask yourself is whether these findings ring true for you in your environment. If they do, I expect you can see why the last thing that your potential customers want is to be talked into purchasing something by a talking sales brochure. In fact, some of them may be more knowledgeable about your products and services than you are.

This changes the customers' expectations of you. They're less interested in listening to you talk about what you sell, and much more interested in exploring how they can use your product or service to benefit their business. You have to understand how it works, not just in theory but in real life.

There's more scrutiny from customers

It's hard to think of a time when our leaders, both corporate and political, were less trusted than they are today. You only have to look at the mainstream media to read about yet another disgraced CEO departing the boardroom with a golden handshake, or a politician accused of using their position to advance their own interests. And because we're all less subservient to authority than we used to be, customers are too. They question you more and trust you less.

This reduced faith in people's integrity also extends into the buying process. Have you wondered why so many more people are involved in it today than they were before? It's because different departments don't always trust each other to make wise decisions. Let's take the following scenario as an example. The VP of Finance in a large organization would like to subscribe to some cloud-based software to make their accounting process more streamlined. They talk to a salesperson at the technology company which provides the software, but then the organization's IT department wants to get involved as well. To say nothing of Procurement, which has been tasked with wielding the stick of frugality now that money is scarce. Of course, in some ways this presents more opportunities for a salesperson, but it also increases complexity and gives them more to juggle. No wonder that a Gartner study showed that in IT, the number of decision-makers involved in the buying process has more than doubled between 2010 and 2020.[5]

Sales teams are under performing

A couple of years ago I spent a while coaching Stuart, a sales manager, who wasn't happy in his role. In between our second and third sessions, he forwarded me an email from his boss on which Stuart had written: 'This is why I'm leaving.' When I read the email, I could see why. It outlined the sales revenue by region for each manager, including Stuart, followed by a blasting criticism of everyone's efforts. Littered with capital letters and exclamation marks (you could almost see the guy jabbing his finger and going red in the face) it was rounded off with this 'motivational' message:

'It's like you're asleep. Fix it. Plain and simple. I know this isn't a "touchy feely" email. If you want, save it for a future exit interview. You are all Sales Managers. Please start forecasting and closing like it.'

While there's no excuse for communications like this, it's true that the complexities I mentioned above are making it more difficult than ever for salespeople to perform well. For a number of years, CSO Insights has carried out a global survey for business-to-business companies, with one of its discoveries being that the average attainment of a salesperson is between 53–57% of their quota. That's pretty miserly, and shows what a tough environment Sales is to work in.[6]

An unforgiving approach to underperformance adds to the perennial challenge of attracting and retaining the best salespeople. What talented sales expert wants to join (or stay with) a team that isn't hitting its targets, with so little understanding of the reasons why? And with forecasting becoming more and more difficult to do accurately because of the uncertain world that you're operating in, how can you know what targets are reasonable in any case? It can feel like an impossible task.

Sales is no picnic in its own right

Sometimes it's easy to forget the challenges inherent in Sales itself. For a start, there's no role in a business more exposed than yours. It's like being the goalkeeper in a football team – everyone knows when you've done a good job, and everyone knows when you've slipped up. In Sales you're judged by your numbers, and often paid by them as well. That might be part of the reason you enjoy the job – there's a simplicity to it, and the exhilaration of receiving a performance-related bonus never wears thin. But what about when your figures aren't so good? You're more likely to be fired for under performance than an employee in any other area of the organization.[7]

Second, Sales doesn't necessarily have the greatest of reputations – we've all heard the jokes about used-car salesmen. Being honest, when someone asks you what you do, does it feel good to say that you work in Sales? In research for his book, *To Sell is Human*, Daniel Pink found that of the 25 adjectives and interjections people used when asked to think about 'sales' or 'selling', 20 had negative connotations like pushy, sleazy, and slimy.[8] Is it any wonder that I've known people to change their job titles to take the 'sales' out of them.

What this means for you

It's not all doom and gloom. Sales has always been – and will continue to be – a fascinating, exciting, and rewarding environment to work in. But it's also important to acknowledge the challenges, because it's our habitual responses to them that are at the root of why we're finding it hard to improve things.

First, we tend to assume that all these difficulties are new, and that new problems require new answers. However, some of the problems have been around for a while, and even for those that haven't, I'm not sure that we need novel solutions all the time. Sometimes it comes down to how we look at change, which can be uncomfortable for anyone. If your organization is constantly responding to shifts in its marketplace, it can make you feel as if you're under threat. And when we feel as if we're being attacked, we don't make wise decisions. We react on instinct without thinking things through, taking short cuts rather than creating solutions that work for the long term.

Second, for sales leaders there's a sense of overwhelm. When there's so much to respond to, you can feel as if you're forever treading water – working hard just to stay afloat. You feel out of control, which compounds your unconscious assumption that something is out to get you. Again, this doesn't lead to calm, long-term decision-making. You'll be tempted to apply a quick fix to the problem immediately in front of you, rather than taking a step back and seeing the big picture.

Focus on what you can control

None of this 'quick fix' thinking is your fault – it's just the way that we humans deal with pressing challenges. But it is important to understand that this is probably what you're doing. The real solution is to focus on what you *can* control, not on what you *can't*. There's little you can do about most of the factors that we've talked about, but there's much that you can do about how you respond to them.

A concept I often use in my training sessions with sales managers is developed from Stephen Covey's Circles of Influence.[9] Imagine three concentric circles; the outermost one is the Circle of Concern, then the Circle of Influence and the innermost one is the Circle of Control.

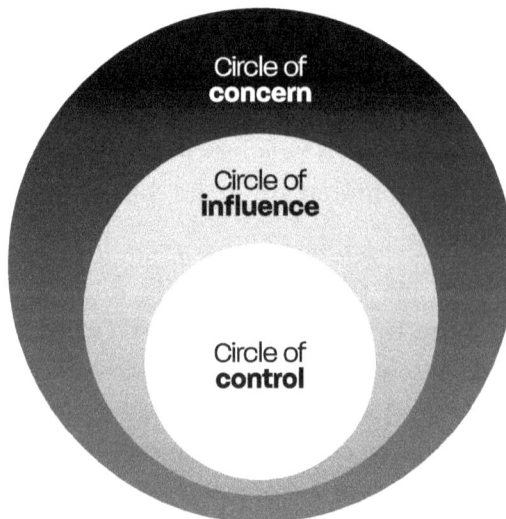

Circle of
concern

Circle of
influence

Circle of
control

The Circle of Concern contains all the external challenges I've talked about, which you can't control. There's no point in worrying about these. The Circle of Control, in the centre, however, contains the things you can directly control, such as how you show up at a meeting or whether you allow yourself to be offended by something. To a degree you can always decide the following: how you respond emotionally to things, where you spend your time and energy, and how you use that energy to change a situation for the better. The Circle of Influence contains the things that you can directly or indirectly impact such as the people you engage with and how things get done. The more you focus on what you can control, the bigger your impact will be on your Circle of Influence.

To take a basic example from everyday life, suppose I've organized a family picnic in the park. My Circle of Concern contains the weather, which I have no control over, but what I can control is my response if it rains. We could move the picnic indoors, change it to another day, or go for a walk in the rain instead. It's up to me how I respond, and the more I focus on my Circles of Influence and Control rather than my Circle of Concern, the better the outcome will be. That's why the sales managers who focus most on what they can control show leadership, while those who feel overwhelmed by what they can't control struggle to make a difference. In fact, the latter group often does a lot of what I call 'BMW' (bitching, moaning, and whinging). This is victimhood, not leadership.

The average tenure of a VP of Sales is 18 months.[10] I find this shocking, because it shows how many sales leaders and managers are giving up (or being given up on). They're not taking control where they can, and it's not just at a senior level, it goes all the way through. Often, when a salesperson leaves their job because of underperformance, it's because they're reacting to their environment rather than looking at what they can control.

Sales must step up. We must recognize that things can be better, despite the challenges, and this starts with identifying what the real problem is.

Your real problem (and it's not what you think it is)

A year ago, I received a call from Anna, the VP of Sales at an online analytics company. A softly spoken woman, she sounded warm and friendly, but I could detect an edge of stress in her voice. 'Our product is a game-changer and should be dominating the market by now, but we're not growing as quickly as we could. The CEO is aiming at a public offering and I'm getting it in the neck to ramp up the sales. We need to develop a stronger pipeline, but my team isn't generating the business. They need training. Can you help?' I replied that I would meet her to see if I could.

As we sat talking over a coffee, I asked Anna some questions about what was going on. She explained that there were multiple teams involved in generating leads for the business, including an external agency, internal partners, and the company's marketing department.

'Do your salespeople see it as their responsibility to generate leads, when there are so many other people doing it?' I asked. 'That's the problem,' she replied. 'They feel uncomfortable about it and would rather wait for the leads to be handed to them. That's why they need training – to make them more confident.'

'I see,' I said. 'And what happens to the leads that those other teams are generating? What's the process for making sure that they reach your salespeople for follow up?' There was a pause. 'Well, there's a system, but I guess it could do with improvement,' she said.

It turned out that the people who were being paid to find the leads were doing a great job, but the leads were falling into a black hole before they arrived at the desks of the salespeople. Training the sales team would never have solved the problem of 'not enough leads.' What Anna had done, just like we all do when we're under pressure, was to assume that the problem was the one she could 'see': a sales team that wasn't generating leads. Her solution was to give them training to do it better, rather than to stand back and analyze the process for the existing lead generators to pass on the leads. As it happened, I did end up carrying out some sales training for Anna's team because I could see that it would have problems coping with all the leads that it was now going to receive, but the training wasn't the core solution.

A quick-fire approach to problem-solving can be as prevalent at the top of an organization as it is at first-line management level, and I liken it to sticking a plaster on a cut. I once worked with a company that had just recruited a new Chief Revenue Officer after the previous one had been fired after three months in the job. 'He wasn't fitting in,' I was told. 'He didn't make enough of an impact straightaway.' After only 12 weeks? That's a sticking-plaster approach, and the reason it's so seductive is because – in the heat of the moment – it feels like the right thing to do. The relief of having an answer that will deliver an instant solution is so powerful that we'll do anything to achieve it, but it almost never works in the long term. Like any sticking-plaster it will eventually fall off, exposing the wound underneath.

What if there was another way? One that involved stepping back and looking at the problem from a wider perspective, so that it could be solved permanently? This is the approach I take when people ask me to deliver sales training for their teams, because in my experience it's not necessarily the performance of the team that's the root cause of the concern. Of course, there are ways that any team can improve, but to go down that route to the exclusion of all else would be to apply a quick fix that wouldn't touch the heart of the issue. Instead, I take a more comprehensive view of the situation. When you do this, you can find yourself uncovering layer after layer of problems until you reach the root cause. It might be that sales training is what's needed, or it might not, but if you don't uncover the real stumbling block to sales success, you'll only be picking up plasters as they drop off over time.

There's another outcome from leaping to fix the problem in front of us straightaway, which is that it's human nature to see the issue as being someone else's fault. If you're honest, isn't it more comfortable to consider the prospect of changing someone else rather than yourself? It's also harder to be objective about yourself than it is about others; it's as if the issue is the nose on your face, and you can't see it until you look in the mirror.

We'll be exploring more about self-development in the next few chapters, but for now this example will help you to see what I mean. I was contacted by Paul, the Head of Sales for a graphic design company with a request for (you guessed it) sales team training. He was new to his position and was coming under pressure from other heads of departments, who were blaming him for the company's problems. Feeling besieged and insecure, he plumped for the most easy and obvious option: improving his team's selling skills. However, when I spent some time with him, I was able to see what was really going on. 'I'm not sure that your sales team is the issue, Paul,' I said. 'Let's take a step back and work it through.'

When we looked at the situation together, it transpired that the problem was more to do with his relationships with the other senior leaders than with his team's capabilities. He began to see that if he could develop a more authoritative and credible relationship with them, he could stop them deflecting their issues onto him. After some coaching in building influence with the right people, he went from strength to strength. It wasn't his team that needed to change, it was him.

The upshot of this is that if you think your problem is complicated because you've not solved it easily and permanently the first time round, it's almost certainly not what you think it is. As Albert Einstein said, 'If I had an hour to solve a problem, I'd spend 55 minutes thinking about the problem and five minutes thinking about solutions.' In other words, he believed that the quality of any solution is only as good as the person's ability to identify the problem they hope to solve. It therefore follows that the key to improving your sales performance is to invest time in defining the problem, as opposed to conjuring up instant solutions to it.

How to discover your real problem

So how do you find the real problem? How do you step back and be objective so that you can see the full breadth of options available to you? There are a number of ways, and you may have your own preferred method, but if you're not sure where to start this process will help.

1. Describe a positive outcome

So often, when we think about solving a problem, we frame it in negative terms. And why wouldn't we? It's a problem, right? But this only makes us feel more stressed about it. If we can describe the outcome we'd like instead, we automatically relax, and this helps our minds to expand and see solutions that would have been hidden before.

> *I want to stop seeing dismal sales reports each month becomes...*
> *I want to feel confident when I present my sales figures to the Board.*
>
> *I want salespeople who don't need their hands holding all the time becomes...*
> *I'd love to have a sales team that's empowered to do its best work.*

The positive frame of mind that this puts you in sets you up for the next step.

2. Reframe your problem

This can be hard, because when you're feeling anxious or threatened it's natural to close in on a problem rather than to take a step back from it. However, it's essential to see the issue from different perspectives. You can start by asking yourself what various people around the organization would see as the concern. How would it appear to:

- ▷ Your boss?
- ▷ Your sales team?
- ▷ Your customers?
- ▷ Any other people who have a vested interest in your sales results?

Write down everything you think that these people would say. Naturally you're only guessing, and you might not know for sure what they think (although you could always ask them), but it helps you to see the issue more widely. Try not to censor your ideas because they seem unviable or imply actions that you wouldn't want to take – at the moment, this list is for your eyes only.

It's also a good idea to remove any emotive language from your answers. When you're matter-of-fact about an issue, it encourages you to think in a rational way and takes away some of the stress. It's a powerful technique. Be specific.

> *I'm struggling to achieve my sales target becomes…*
> *My sales target was x and I achieved y.*
>
> *My boss thinks I'm useless becomes…*
> *My boss expects x, y, and z of me and I'm delivering a, b, and c.*

3. Look for the potential root causes

Write down as many potential causes as possible. Then dig deeper. For each possible cause ask yourself why that happened. Ask again, and keep asking yourself 'why' until you get to the root cause.

Let's take forecast accuracy as an example. There could be many reasons *why* you have a problem hitting your forecast each quarter. One reason is that some of your salespeople are forecasting deals and then moving them out to the following quarter. *Why* are they doing this? Turns out the customer isn't ready to sign and still has a number of actions to complete in their sign-off process. *Why* was the opportunity showing as closing this quarter? The salesperson wasn't aware of the customer's sign-off process and hadn't asked about it. They believed and hoped the deal would close sooner. *Why* didn't they explore this earlier? They feel pressure to maintain a full pipeline and to commit certain deals. It feels easier for them to call their forecast and then slip deals at the end of the quarter rather than face increased scrutiny and challenge throughout the quarter. Therefore, they don't ask questions that they might not like the answer to. *Why* do they think this is okay? Because you tolerate it. You are just like them. You don't ask the right questions early in the process, you accept what they say, and, like them, you hope things are going to turn out well. *Why?*

This is just an example to illustrate the approach. At each stage you may find there are multiple paths you can follow. It is important to explore all of these. You will know that you have revealed the root cause when you can go no further and asking 'why' doesn't give you any meaningful insight.

4. Filter and prioritize your problems

You might find that you end up with a list of problems, when you started with only one. For instance, *I find it hard to attract the right people and I also have a problem retaining them. On top of that, I need to understand more about lead generation*. This can feel dispiriting, but it's actually a good sign because it shows that you're seeing the situation more broadly. And it's almost always the case that when a problem keeps coming up and seems hard to fix, there are layers of issues to deal with rather than just one.

The next thing is to decide which problems you're going to tackle now, and which you'll leave for another time. Let's take a leaf out of Warren Buffett's book here; as one of the most successful businesspeople in the world, he obviously knows a thing or two about focus and prioritization. He once had a long-serving pilot, Mike Flint, who flew his private plane. They were having a conversation about career and life ambitions, and Buffett asked Flint to write down his top goals. Flint returned with a list of 25 goals. When he saw the list, Buffett said, 'Out of those 25, I want you to pick your top five.' So, Flint came back with five. Then Buffett said to him, 'What about the others on the list? The other 20?' Flint's response was, 'They're pretty important to me as well, so when I find time, I'll fit them in.' To this Buffett said, 'No you don't. You don't think about the others until you've achieved your top five goals. The reason we don't get things done is that we try to achieve too many of them, rather than focusing on the most important.'[11]

If you have various problems, which one is the top priority? Which one will make the most difference if you could solve it? Focus on that before addressing anything else. The same goes while you're reading this book. You might find yourself thinking, 'Hey, that idea might work for me,' but please don't try to action too many of them. Focus on just one and get it working for you, refining it as needed, and then move to the next one. If you try to do too much, you'll feel overwhelmed, and before you know it, you'll be back where you started. Concentrate instead on the one or two things that will create the most significant impact.

5. Turn towards yourself

Now you know which problem you're going to tackle; it's time to look to yourself. It's easy to assume that other people are responsible for whatever's going wrong, but without you making some inner changes nothing will transform over the longer term. You can ask yourself these questions.

- What have I done that's contributed to this problem?

- What have I not done?

- Do I genuinely want to solve this problem?

- What am I prepared to do about it?

This process isn't easy, but it's so much more effective than applying a sticking-plaster. When you take the time to articulate what's happening from a wider perspective, you'll find that a light bulb goes on. What was once a mystery will become clear, and you'll feel confident that your time and effort will now be spent in the right place.

In the next chapter we'll explore the true nature of sales leadership, and how you can apply it to your own situation in order to grow from a manager to a leader.

Key takeaways

- Sales professionals face unprecedented challenges in a volatile and complex business landscape.

- The instinct to apply quick fixes often masks deeper, underlying problems that require attention.

- Effective problem-solving begins with stepping back, reframing issues, and identifying root causes.

- Focusing on controllable factors, rather than external concerns, fosters impactful and sustainable solutions.

- Personal reflection and prioritization are critical to driving meaningful change and overcoming obstacles.

Chapter 2

It starts with you

Let's imagine a couple of scenarios. In the first, you have a sales team made up of the usual mix of talents: a couple of superstars, another couple who look as if they'll be heading for the exit soon, and the majority who are somewhere in the middle. The superstars can take care of themselves, and the laggards just need managing out. It's the mediocre bunch in between that's the problem. They're great at following-up leads and managing the sales process up to a certain point, but their challenge is with closing sales – they just can't seem to do it. So, when you sense that their deals are going too slowly and are worried they might be lost, you have to step in and finalize them yourself. It's not ideal because by the time you get to them some are beyond saving, but at least you manage to scrape across the finish line most quarters.

In the second scenario, the organization you work for is stuck in the dark ages, with paperwork ruling the day. Every sale your team makes has to be reported to multiple departments, you can't hire anyone new without jumping through hoops, and as for firing someone for underperformance – forget it. HR would have a nervous breakdown. No wonder you struggle to meet your targets when you're weighed down by all this bureaucracy. The company needs to be more agile, empowering its people to make their own decisions. If everyone spent less time filling out forms and more time talking to customers, sales would go up. And if you could have the freedom to pick and choose your team the way you want, who knows where you could take the business? It's such a shame that no-one can see that.

In each of these situations, the cause of the problems with sales seems obvious. In the first it's salespeople who can't close deals. Naturally this affects your figures, and given that the team members in question aren't bad enough to fire, you have no option but to plug the gaps. In the second scenario the issue is a stagnant, bureaucratic culture. No wonder your team loses opportunities when they have to fill in a form for every customer visit – it puts them off reaching out to speculative contacts. And when people don't feel trusted, they don't perform.

And yet, these aren't the reasons for the poor sales. So, given that we've seen what happens when we jump to conclusions, let's take a moment to think this through.

In the first scenario the salespeople lack confidence with closing deals. But how are they supposed to learn to do it better when their manager is always jumping in and taking over? After a while they come to expect it, so that even when they do have a go, they have a sneaking suspicion their boss would make a better job of it than they could. In the second example, the salespeople are weighed down by paperwork. But their manager, instead of challenging the elements of it that aren't necessary and explaining the importance of the parts that are, joins in the chorus of moaning.

In each of these situations it's the *management and leadership* of the sales team that's the cause of the problem, not the sales team itself. This is good news, because changing yourself is within your control, whereas changing other people is a whole lot harder. And it's why this chapter explores the purpose of management and leadership in a sales environment, so that you can see how you can make a significant difference in the way you lead your team.

The hardest thing to admit

Remember Robert, the VP of Sales of the large manufacturing company from the Introduction? His company sold industrial uniforms to various types of workplaces, with each salesperson having their own territory containing a number of different customer types. They would identify potential customers, contact them to make appointments, and visit them to sell their products.

'Do you know what the best salespeople in your company are like?' I asked. 'What they do, how they do it, and the skills they have?'

'Not really', he replied. 'The problem is', I explained, 'that if you bring in the best people from elsewhere, but they have different characteristics to the ones who perform best in your organization, they won't necessarily do well. For instance, if they're great at selling to a prospect who's been given to them as a lead, but poor at spotting opportunities in the first place, they might struggle.'

Robert's face changed as he started to see that he might have been better off recruiting people who were similar to those who performed best in his own company, rather than simply looking at who'd sold the most in other organizations – even if they were in the same sector. In other words, it was his recruitment strategy that was a key part of the issue.

Robert's attitude to these salespeople was similar to how many sales managers respond when faced with performance issues. They think that their teams need to be improved, either through skills development or by replacing the people within them: *change* the people or change the *people*. Training and firing feel tangible and visible, but they're a way of abdicating responsibility for the real problem.

Sometimes it's the hardest thing in the world to admit that *we're* the problem. That as leaders we're responsible for enabling our teams to achieve great things, and that if those teams are unsuccessful that it might not be entirely down to the people within them. In Robert's case his low sales were caused by him recruiting the wrong people, not by the people being wrong in themselves. In someone else's case it might be down to a lack of guidance and inspiration for their team. The point is that it's the leader who needs to change, not just the individual salespeople.

The difference between leadership and management

So far, I've been using the words 'leader' and 'manager' almost interchangeably. However, now that we're looking at the role of a sales manager in more depth, it's time to acknowledge that there's a difference between the two – although it's not necessarily the one you might think. Often the way that the words 'leader' and 'manager' are referenced implies that that leadership is good, and management is bad, as if they're the Luke Skywalker and Darth Vader of the business world. But it's not the destiny of leadership to defeat management – in fact, they're two sides of the same coin. They're different but complementary skill sets, and in an increasingly complex and continuously changing world, one can't function without the other.

The purpose of management is to allocate your resources so that your salespeople can achieve their objectives and your organization its goals. It's a role: a position you hold. In that sense anyone who has responsibility for anyone else is a manager, even if the manager is a CEO or senior executive. Leadership, on the other hand, isn't a role or position – it's an element of what you do as a manager, and is a skill you can learn. This is different from how it's often seen, with leaders holding the most senior positions and managers being below them.

So, what is leadership? It's the ability to influence people through articulating a purpose and vision, motivating and inspiring them to achieve a goal. It's not an additional step on the hierarchy, but an approach you take to your management role that will help you to achieve what you want. Leadership is what makes the difference between being a good manager and a great one, so to be the best sales manager you can be you have to recognize that leadership is a key part of what you do.

Leadership also takes a longer-term view of a situation, rather than jumping to a short-term fix. As such, you can see how integral it is to your role as a manager in terms of identifying the real source of your sales problem. Unfortunately, people are often rewarded for the wrong things, and this is particularly true in sales. Managers are promoted or given bonuses purely because of their short-term results, and not on whether they're likely to achieve their long-term objectives.

It's true to say that most organizations are over-managed and under-led, and that effective leadership skills are in short supply. The 2015 Brandon Hall Group's *State of Leadership Development Study* reveals that 71% of respondents think their leaders aren't ready to lead their organizations into the future. Filling this skills gap should be a critical priority for the majority of businesses.

The crisis in leadership wouldn't be so concerning if the leadership development programmes that many organizations are developing were fit for purpose. The unfortunate reality, though, is that they tend to be management training courses disguised as leadership courses. They focus on mitigating or eliminating risk, improving efficiencies, and creating process and measurement methodologies. These are all management activities, and while they're important, doing what you've always done but more efficiently is not on its own a recipe for success.

Think about how you spend your time on a day-to-day basis. Planning? Budgeting? Monitoring and coordinating your team's activities? Reporting on progress? Putting in place fixes when things go off track? This is management, and it needs to be done. But it's not leadership – it's not what will make you a *great* manager. It might be that you're focusing on these activities because you work in an organization that has a management, rather than a leadership, culture. You do what you see others do, and you're rewarded for it. That's perfectly understandable, but it won't stop you being the problem. For that you need to develop leadership skills.

An awkward transition

How did you get into sales? I often ask people this question, and more often than not the answer runs along the lines of, 'Well, I fell into it really.' There was a poll on LinkedIn that showed the same, with over 80% of sales specialists giving a similar answer. That's not to say that many salespeople don't enjoy their jobs and aren't good at them, but Sales was never a deliberate career choice for them.

I tend to find that moving from individual salesperson to sales manager follows the same process – it's something that happens because it's the obvious next step. Again, there's nothing wrong with that in itself, but it does mean that you might not have thought through the different skills you'll need as a leader to the ones you had as a contributor. When change is unconscious, competence rarely follows automatically – it takes new thinking to achieve it.

When I first met Stuart, the recipient of the terrible email I mentioned in the last chapter, he was a newly promoted sales manager. As is the case for so many like him, he'd previously been a top-performing salesperson. However, things weren't going so well for him now. As an individual salesperson his sole focus had been to hit or exceed his targets, so he was skilled at managing his time and energy, and at short-term problem solving. If a customer had an issue, he'd drop everything to deal with it, and he could choose how hard he worked to make that happen.

The problem arose when he employed the same tactics as a manager. Every time one of his team came up against a barrier he'd jump in and fix it for them, which took away opportunities for them to learn and develop. It also wasn't scalable, which meant that his time was increasingly taken up with doing his people's jobs for them. This led him to adopt a command-and-control style of leadership, in which he'd tell people what to do because he didn't have the time to coach them so they could solve the problem themselves, which led to them asking him for help all the time, which led to… You can see how the situation was spiralling out of control.

It's what's called the Peter Principle, a management concept developed by Laurence Peter in which people are promoted based on their success in previous jobs until they reach a level at which they're no longer competent. Skills in one role don't necessarily translate to another.

Have you experienced this kind of negative cycle? Take a moment to ask yourself the following questions:

> ▷ The last few times I helped one of my team with a problem, what did I do?

> ▷ How long did it take me?

- Did I enjoy the process, or find it frustrating?

- Did the person learn anything about how to deal with something similar next time?

- What kind of manager would the person have described me as after the interaction I had with them?

Your role as a leader isn't to do other people's jobs for them, it's to make it possible for them to do a great job for themselves. Your success comes from the sum efforts of your team, not your individual sales figures.

You may think that this sounds all well and good, but that empowering people takes time. You're under pressure and don't have the hours in the day to sit down with people explaining things, when a quick command or direct call to a customer would achieve the same results. You need sales, and fast. I get that, which is why later in the book you'll learn ways of leading and coaching which won't take up extra time – I promise. But for now, just be open to the idea that one of the reasons you're busy is because you're carrying other people's baggage for them. It can be a hard habit to break. The thrill of closing the deal, the rapport with customers – it's part of what made your old job as a salesperson so much fun. But to be a great sales manager you have to recognize that the skills you need now are different, and when you develop them, they'll bring their own rewards.

In the next chapter we'll look in more detail at what it means to be a great sales manager and learn some useful things about leadership that will make a concrete difference to the results you achieve.

Key takeaways

- Sales issues often originate from shortcomings in management and leadership, not just team performance.

- Effective management involves resource allocation and process efficiency to achieve team objectives.

- Leadership inspires and motivates teams by articulating a clear purpose and vision.

▶ Transitioning from salesperson to manager requires developing new skills and adapting to a broader, team-focused perspective.

▶ Success as a manager depends on enabling your team to perform independently, rather than solving problems for them.

Chapter 3
The journey, not the destination

A few years ago, I ran a sales leadership workshop in the beautiful city of San Francisco. A friend and colleague of mine, Michael, was supporting me with it, and shared a story from his early career as a sales manager that has stuck with me ever since. Michael was having a conversation with his mentor, Asma, shortly after taking up the role. She asked him how the job was going, and Michael said that it seemed to be okay. He talked her through what he'd done and how he'd gone about it. The insight came from what she asked him next.

'What do you think would happen, Michael, if your sales team was to decide how much you're paid each month? If they were given complete discretion to write out any cheque they liked based purely on what value you've given to them individually? What would be the result? How much would you earn?'

The role of a sales manager is not to do a salesperson's job for them, but to help them develop the skills and capabilities to be the best that they can be, and to continue to grow. It's like enhancing their personal stock value, much like the stocks and shares of a company. The rewards that team members pay should be based on how much the manager has helped increase their personal stock value, rather than just on whether they helped them close some deals. When a manager enhances the personal stock value of their team members, they become more committed, engaged, and motivated to achieve greater success, resulting in increased overall success for the team and the company.

This was genius, because it brought home to Michael that the core purpose of his role as a manager was to bring value to his team by developing them so that they could achieve better sales on their own, and that *this* is what should be rewarded. How much more committed, engaged, and motivated is the salesperson who writes out a high pay cheque? How much more are they prepared to do for the manager who inspires and supports them? And how much less energized is the one who pays a low amount? You could try asking yourself the same question as Asma asked Michael – I'd be amazed if you didn't come up with some interesting answers.

Asma gave one more piece of honest (and somewhat brutal) advice before she left. She explained to Michael that he was a good *deal* manager but that he had some way to go before he became a good *sales* manager. In other words, he hadn't made the transition from being an individual contributor to being a leader. He was skilled in – and enjoyed – helping his people to close deals, but he wasn't leading them in a way that enabled them to do it for themselves. And herein lies the challenge that every sales manager faces when they transition from being a salesperson.

Are you a deal manager or a sales manager? Here are some questions to ask yourself.

1. What percentage of your people are currently on or above plan?

    a. Less than 25%

    b. 50%

    c. 75% and above

2. What do you do with under performers?

    a. Tolerate them

    b. Manage them out

    c. Coach them to improve

3. What type of pipeline activity attracts most of your attention?

   a. Deal negotiation and closing

   b. Progressing mid-stage opportunities

   c. Top of funnel/demand generation

4. What timeframe do you typically focus your deal reviews?

   a. Current month

   b. Current quarter

   c. Next quarter plus

5. How would you describe your general coaching style?

   a. Directing (explaining how something should be done)

   b. Guiding (offering suggestions on how something could be done)

   c. Enabling (encouraging self-discovery and ownership)

Results aren't everything

The distinction between a deal manager and a sales manager highlights the emphasis that many people place on results, as opposed to what contributed to those results – the decisions, the coaching, and all the other elements a leader brings. This misplaced focus is the crux of the issue that we face in sales leadership today. Deal managers see achieving good results as the most important element of their jobs, whereas sales leaders care deeply about results also, but view them as the outcome of a series of actions. They recognize that results are the end point of a journey, not a destination in their own right. Let me just clarify this, results are important but how we get the results is equally, if not more, important.

A focus on results is understandable because when you think about how you're judged, it's mainly on your sales figures. It's natural to do whatever you can to make sure that you hit your targets in the short term. I'm sure that you wouldn't relish a conversation with your boss in which you defend your low sales on the basis of having done a lot of team development this quarter. However, that's not what I'm talking about. Results will always be important, but if your people achieve them at the cost of being able to think for themselves, you'll create a number of crippling issues.

Uneven performance within your team

A deal manager is only concerned with their team hitting its overall target. To them, it's not a problem if some people under perform as long as there are enough overachievers to make up the difference. Even a salesperson on 30% of their quota is contributing something to the overall number! A sales manager, however, knows it's important that *each* person in the team hits or exceeds their goals, and if everyone isn't doing this they ask themselves why. Think what it would do to your figures if all members of your team were working at the same level as the ones who are your success stories today. It would be transformational.

Another aspect of this is that when you have people who aren't hitting their targets, you'll find that they tend to leave after a while, either because you manage them out or because they depart of their own accord. This can prompt questions about your staff turnover due to the money it costs to hire and onboard people. Far better to be known as a leader for whom people actively want to work because you offer the opportunity to grow, than a manager they're lucky to last a year with.

Short-term thinking

A deal manager is constantly looking at the ground to make sure they don't trip over, whereas a sales manager looks at the horizon. When you concentrate only on what's in front of you, your sales will peak and trough, peak and trough. Eventually they might fall off a cliff. When you habitually look further ahead, however, your transition from one quarter to another is smoother. You'll be prepared for whatever happens, because you'll know what's in your pipeline as well as what's on the table. And you'll have ensured that your pipeline is a quality one which contributes to where your organization wants to be in the future, rather than just today.

Deal managers are busiest towards the end of the sales process, helping to close deals. They will do everything to help their salespeople close what is in their sights. This is typified by the frenzied rush of activity at the end of each month. The danger of this is they may miss the bigger opportunity. It leaves little chance to influence the deal in terms of size and scope. Sales managers invest at the beginning of the process. They help their salespeople put plans in place not only to progress deals to closure but to build a robust, healthy pipeline of opportunities. They then support their people to execute their plans and take steps towards sustainable growth.

Not knowing what works

This is the big one. When you're focused only on results, you never know if what your team achieves is down to luck – good or bad. Even a turkey can fly as long as the wind is behind them; it's when it drops that difficulties arise. I've known salespeople who looked, on paper, as if they were high performers, but who were probably just in the right place at the right time due to the customers they had or the territory they worked. Likewise, I've known salespeople who appeared to fail at their jobs but who were actually just as competent as those who achieved better results. Firing them or managing them out didn't solve the sales problem, it just felt as if it would.

This is why knowing what causes results is as important as the results themselves, because otherwise you can't replicate them, build on them, or enable others in your team to achieve them. When you have a team that's high-performing because all the people in it know what they're doing, it's repeatable and sustainable in the long-term.

The same goes for decision-making. The quality of your decisions isn't determined by the decisions themselves, but by how you reach them. When you know what that process is, you've created transferable knowledge. I remember being in a lesson at school and being asked a question that I didn't know the answer to. Not wanting to expose my ignorance, I hazarded a guess. 'Well done!' said the teacher. 'You're right.' Even at that age I was aware that I hadn't learned anything – I only looked as if I had.

This plays out across Sales in all sorts of ways. There are too many deal managers – rather than sales managers – at all levels, because organizations reward the wrong things: results. If you're a Chief Revenue Officer or VP of Sales, are you recruiting and promoting deal managers? And are you doing this simply because of the results they've achieved? Or are you aware of what's needed to become a *sales* manager – a great one? When you're hiring a sales manager, the first line of their job description should be: 'To achieve your goals through the development of your people,' not 'To achieve sales targets.' You want that manager to know what it takes to get great results, not to rely on their past luck without realizing it.

This dovetails with the direction that businesses are moving in today. On both a consumer and a corporate level, people increasingly care about corporate social responsibility and the effect that organizations have on their communities. They're less tolerant of corporate wrongdoing and pay more attention to how companies achieve their results, as opposed to only the results themselves. What's more, this is good for business. Companies with a commitment to nurturing people far outlast those that only concentrate on profit, and they are more successful.

As a manager, you have a huge responsibility not just to your organization but for the impact you have on the people you lead. I've come across many managers who make their decisions based on themselves rather than others, and this is what leads to the macho and self-centred culture that can exist in Sales today. When you're an individual contributor you can afford to focus only on yourself, but as a manager that shouldn't be an option. Not only is it morally wrong, but you'll be unlikely to create long-term sales success.

'How' is as important as 'What'

Quantifying your results is easy, simply look at the goals you set at the beginning of the year and determine whether you have moved the needle on those goals. Determining the *quality* and means of your results requires a much deeper and rigorous self-assessment. I'd like you to think back to your most recent set of sales figures. Ask yourself the following question:

> *What specific things did I do, or not do, that directly contributed to those results?*

You can focus on behaviours, actions, decisions, and attitudes – anything that points you towards your contribution to your sales figures, rather than the figures themselves. Please give it a go.

Researcher and leadership expert Liz Wiseman has identified three types of behaviours that managers can exhibit: Accelerating Behaviours, Blocking Behaviours, and Neutral Behaviours.[1] Accelerating Behaviours are actions that create an environment where team members can perform at their best and achieve more than they thought possible. Blocking Behaviours, on the other hand, are actions that get in the way of team members' success and limit their potential. Neutral Behaviours are actions that do not actively support nor hinder team members' progress. While not harmful, they do not contribute to the growth of the team either.

As a sales manager, it's important to reflect on your own behaviours and identify where you fall on this spectrum. Do your actions accelerate the growth and potential of your team members, or do they block it? Or are they simply neutral? Be honest, what would actually happen if you weren't there? By understanding the impact of your behaviours, you can begin to make changes that will multiply the capability of your team and help them reach their full potential.

High-growth versus high-performance culture

Some organizations love to talk about the fact that they have a 'high-performance culture.' It makes them sound as if they're packed with over-achievers who are raring to smash their targets and send their businesses soaring into the stratosphere. However, sustainable performance can only be achieved as a result of *growth* – or having a high-growth culture. In other words, it's growth that leads to great results.

So, what is a high-growth culture?[2] It's one in which people are encouraged to develop themselves in all sorts of ways. This could be through sharpening their professional skills, understanding how they operate on a personal level so they can regulate how they respond to problems, and learning how to get the best out of their colleagues and customers.

A high-growth business is the product of a growth (rather than a fixed) mindset in its employees. You may be familiar with the work of renowned psychologist Carol Dweck on the importance of having a growth mindset.[3] What she discovered through her research was that people with a growth mindset understand their abilities not to be fixed but to be improvable through effort. This leads them to seek out, and thrive on, challenges because they know that this is how they'll become better. They're adaptable, proactive, and enthusiastic, enjoying the process of learning and improving. As a result, they perform far better than those who assume they have an innate level of ability that can never change.

In contrast, a performance-driven culture tends to brand people as winners and losers. Who's made the most sales this quarter? Who's employee of the month? This creates an atmosphere in which everyone focuses on what other people think of them by competing for recognition and rewards, and there's less attention paid to any good work that's being done regardless of results. In a high-growth culture it's not that results don't matter, but that they're seen as the culmination of the many actions that led to them. It's those decisions that we should pay attention to if we're to learn from what worked and what didn't.

It isn't necessarily easy to create a high-growth culture in your team because it involves people (including yourself) admitting that they don't know it all – that they make mistakes and want to learn from them. You have to make a conscious decision to prioritize professional growth over a results-at-all-costs approach, so that you can create a basis for long-term and sustainable change.

The interplay between results and values

If you want to create a transformational shift from scraping your target each quarter to sailing past it every time, you have to move away from the idea that your role is only to improve on what you already do. Incremental refinement is a management mindset. It takes *leadership* to set a new vision and inspire people to work towards it.

There's been much research carried out in recent years about how leaders can best do this. A study was carried out by David Ulrich of the University of Michigan, together with consultants Jack Zenger and Norm Smallwood.[4] They argue that for a leader to be effective they need to possess certain characteristics, such as analytical thinking, the ability to work with ambiguity, and personal integrity. But they also need to know how to connect these leadership attributes to the results they achieve. The authors of the research recommend that leaders should continually ask themselves what's required for bringing about the right results, and tell stories around the organization about how they accomplished them. Note that this isn't *that* they accomplished them, but *how*. There's even a formula that came out of this:

$$\text{Effective Leadership} = \text{Attributes} \times \text{Results}$$

This equation shows that leaders should both demonstrate the right attributes and achieve results, with each factor multiplying the other. For instance, a score of 2 out of 10 in attributes multiplied by a score of 9 out of 10 in results gives an effectiveness rating of only 18 out of 100. Whereas a score of 8 out of 10 in attributes multiplied by a score of 5 out 10 on results gives a higher effectiveness rating of 40 out of 100.

This underlines the fact that results are important – vital even. But so is the value-set that enables them to be achieved. Ulrich offers four criteria for judging whether leaders are focused on delivering results in a sustainable way. You can see how the end outcome is about far more than beating a quarterly target.

- ▹ Balanced – do the results balance the needs of different groups within the organization, ignoring no-one?

- ▹ Strategic – do the results link to the organization's overall strategy?

> ▷ Lasting – do the results meet short-term goals without sacrificing long-term ones?

> ▷ Selfless – do the results support the whole business, and not just the individual manager's personal objectives?

Another piece of research, carried out by Bradley University in the US, reinforces the philosophy of Jack Welch, who was CEO of General Electric at the time of the study.[5] Welch was an advocate of what was called the Performance-Values Matrix, which shows that when leaders do their work in a way that exemplifies the values of the organization, this leads to high levels of performance and sustained growth. If attention is only paid to one of these, the same success won't be achieved.

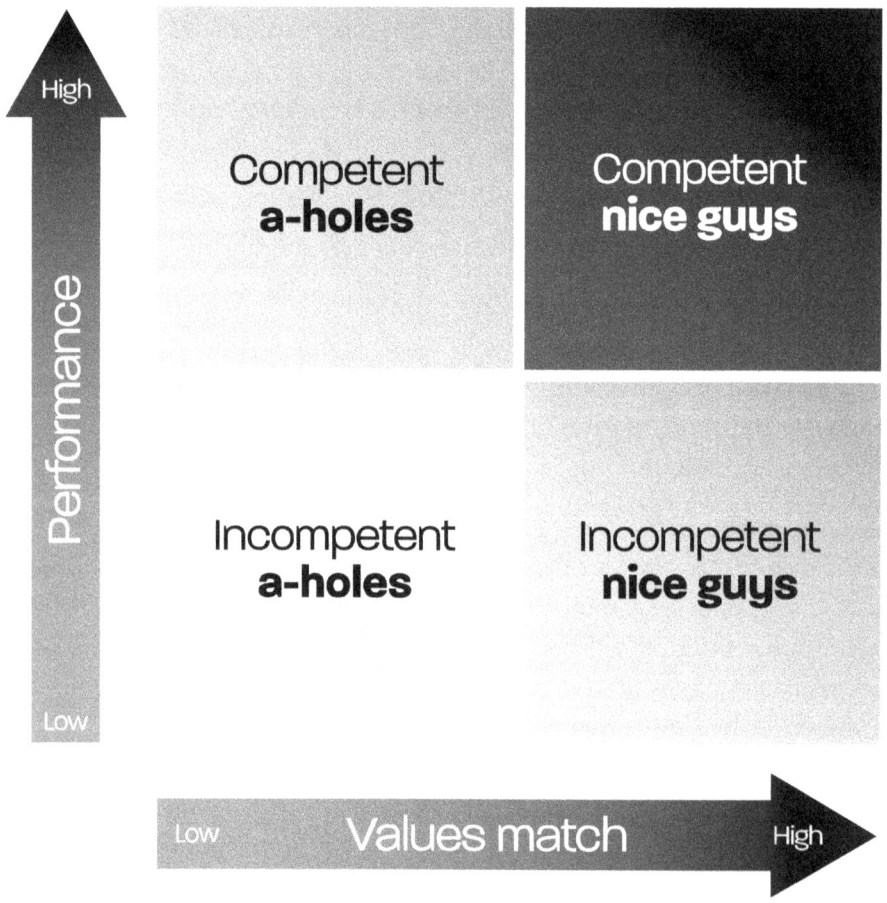

This model (called The Performance-Values Matrix) is important because it shows that, while it's possible to be a high achiever because of the circumstances you happen to be in, it's only when you know how you're creating your success that you can repeat it and be adaptable. I'd rather manage a salesperson who knows why they've achieved what they have than someone who's been lucky. The former can replicate their results whereas the latter can't.

And yet I often come across sales managers who say that they don't mind if they have a couple of mavericks on their team who don't embody the values of the business, as long as they massively over perform while they're about it. I wonder what their CEO would say if they heard that? Some may call these people mavericks; others may call them a-holes. These are people who can get results, but they do it their way regardless of the consequences to the rest of the business; the ends justify the means so to say. But what effect does it have on the rest of the sales team and wider organization? To tolerate this situation is to have a deal manager mindset, in which all that matters is closing the next sale regardless of the wider impact. The mess that these people leave behind is no fun to clear up, either for you or the rest of your team.

You've learned a lot about what it takes to be a great sales manager – even a leader – and you may be feeling a little daunted about whether you're up to the challenge. Fear not. In the next chapter, we'll look at how you can develop your own potential for leadership, because you have it in you be a leader – you just need to understand what to do.

Key takeaways

- Deal managers focus on closing deals themselves, often at the expense of their team's growth and independence.

- Sales Leaders foster a growth mindset, enabling their team to learn, develop, and achieve sustainable success.

- Understanding and replicating the processes behind results is key to building long-term performance.

▶ High-growth cultures prioritize personal and professional development, leading to consistent and scalable high performance.

▶ Leaders who align their actions with organizational values create results that are balanced, strategic, lasting, and selfless.

Chapter 4
The secret to confident leadership

You're sitting in your airline seat awaiting take off, wondering how long it will be before you can open your laptop and work on your latest sales proposal. Along comes the air steward to give you the required pre-flight briefing and safety demonstration. After explaining the features of the aircraft and what will happen in the case of an emergency, they tell you that, in the event of a loss of cabin pressure, oxygen masks will drop from the overhead compartment. And if you're traveling with children, what do they always advise? Put on your own mask before helping anyone else. Because if you become incapacitated, you're of no use to anyone.

The same applies to leadership: you can't lead others if your own thinking is impaired. You don't need charisma, personal magnetism, or a bunch of other fancy personality traits, but you do need to behave in a way that inspires trust and enthusiasm. And yet defining a purpose for your team, and instilling the belief that it can be achieved, doesn't come easily to everyone, which is why it's helpful to explore how you feel about yourself. Your behaviour is determined by your thinking, which is in turn created by your beliefs about what kind of person you are. So, while leadership is really about others, paradoxically, you have to look to yourself first.

Central to leadership is feeling secure and confident in your ability to lead. We all struggle to some extent with insecurity and what's often called 'imposter syndrome', the notion that we don't deserve to be in our jobs and will one day be 'found out'. So, let's try to alleviate some of the concerns that you may be having and stretch your imagination at the same time. And while some of what you'll learn here may make you feel a little uncomfortable, that's okay. Because as well as being the problem, you're also the solution.

As well as being about you, this chapter is also about happiness. I meet many sales managers and leaders who feel unfulfilled and stressed by their roles. Part of this is down to the overwhelm I've talked about already, but there's more to it than that. I have a sense that they're not sure what would help them to enjoy their jobs, because they don't know what success looks like for them. And while success and happiness aren't the same thing, there's definitely a link between them. You don't have to be successful to be happy, but I'm convinced that if you're happy you're more likely to be successful.

What sort of leader do you want to be?

As we've already explored, many people fall into sales without planning to, and if that's the case for you, you might not have given much thought to what kind of sales leader you want to be. That's natural, but if you're not sure what sort of leader you are, how can you lead with consistency and conviction? Your leadership style will likely be swayed by the problems and personalities you come across from day to day, which won't instil much confidence in your team. You might also fall into the trap of following on from what your predecessor did because it's what everyone expects, rather than deciding on your own style and approach.

The sort of leader you are should stem from the kind of person you are. People can always tell when you're trying to be someone you're not. You'll enjoy your role more, and be better at it, when your leadership style is congruent with your personality. It therefore stands to reason that it's a good idea to get to know yourself better, and you can do this by examining your values, strengths, and motivations.

Your values

A few months after leaving the relative safety of employment, and while I was still building my sales leadership coaching business, I received two attractive opportunities. One was an all-expenses-paid trip to Paris with a company I was doing associate work with. It promised to be a fun couple of days away and would give me networking opportunities to help grow my profile. The other was from someone who was wanting a co-trainer for their one-day training event. Unlike the Paris trip it was paid, which at the time was a big deal to me. However, the dates for each opportunity clashed so the question was, which option would I take? The excitement of Paris and building future opportunities or the immediate financial reward of the training day?

The answer was that I did neither. Why? Because both events ran on my middle daughter's birthday, and I've never missed a single one of my children's birthdays. I've always been there in the morning to open their presents with them when they wake up, and light the candles on their cake at teatime. Of course, I could have come up with plenty of reasons to go: I needed the money, my daughter would be at school all day in any case, and we could celebrate at the weekend. But this was a values-based decision, and as soon as I saw the dates I knew what I would do.

My choice may not have been the same as yours would have been, but that doesn't matter. The point is that I knew what was most important to me and therefore had no dilemma about what path to take. Our personal values drive much of our behaviour and decision-making, and when we struggle with making decisions it can often be because there's an unacknowledged conflict with our values.

It follows that to understand ourselves, we need to know what our values are. This can be difficult to assess, because while our values may appear obvious to others, to ourselves they can be hidden. Here's a way of helping you to reach a deeper understanding of your most significant values. To evaluate what matters most to you in life, answer the questions below as thoughtfully as possible.

> Think about three people whom you admire. What is it about them that you respect? This will give you a clue as to which values you find aspirational.

- What quality, trait, or attribute do people compliment you on the most? How do others describe you? Your values often reveal themselves in how you behave.

- When do you feel most authentically 'you'? Conversely, when do you feel most like a fraud? What's happening in each of these situations?

- Which three things can you absolutely not tolerate? Which three people do you most dislike, and why? What are you prepared to fight against or stand up to?

- What kinds of things inspire you to take action?

Having given these questions some consideration, turn to the List of Core Values at the end of the book and select 20 that are most important to you. Now start to narrow down your list until you have only ten remaining; you might find that there are some pairings or groups that will help you with this process.

Next, put your ten remaining values in order of importance to you. All of them are a big deal, but which are paramount? Which would you fight for and refuse to give up on? Cross out the bottom seven. How do you feel about the remaining top three? Do they inform your decision-making, determine what you do, and inspire you?

Your only remaining step is to show your final three values to someone who knows you well, because it can be tempting to choose the ones that you would like to think you have, rather than the ones that actually drive your behaviour. Would other people be able to observe your values in what you say and do? Is there clear evidence that these values are what motivates you in most aspects of your life?

Understanding and identifying your personal values as a sales leader is crucial. They guide your decisions, actions, and leadership style, fostering trust and credibility with your team. Clarifying your values brings clarity, authenticity, and integrity to your leadership. It empowers you to navigate challenges and make tough decisions aligned with your core beliefs. By embodying your values, you create a purpose-driven sales culture that inspires exceptional results from your team.

While personal values provide a strong foundation for sales leadership, it's crucial to recognize that certain values can hinder our progress and conflict with our objectives. It is essential to continuously evaluate and work on aligning our values with our desired outcomes. By acknowledging and addressing any conflicting values, we can proactively seek personal growth and development. This self-reflection allows us to overcome potential obstacles, adapt our approach, and refine our leadership style to better serve our team and achieve our collective goals. Embracing this growth mindset enables us to evolve as sales leaders and create a more harmonious and successful environment.

One value that comes up time and again for salespeople is competitiveness. In my experience this is not a particularly helpful one for a leader to have, because it involves focusing on yourself rather than others. You don't have to stop being a competitive person, but you do need to recognize that it might get in the way of being an effective leader. I'll admit that I'm a very competitive person myself and, looking back on my career, I can see that there were many occasions on which it didn't serve me well. I would sometimes put the interests of my own team before others in the business, just so that I could say I'd pipped them to the post.

In an enlightening study published in *Journal of Personal Selling and Sales Management*,[1] different forms of competitive focus were identified, shedding light on their varying impact on motivation and team dynamics in sales. By encouraging salespeople to shift their focus from *Inter*personal Competitiveness, where they compete with those they work with, to *Intra*personal Competitiveness, where they compete against their own past performance or personal best, and to direct their attention towards the external competitors they face, leaders can foster a more productive and cohesive sales environment. This approach allows salespeople to strive for personal improvement while maintaining a collaborative atmosphere, ultimately leading to increased motivation and stronger team dynamics.

There are better ways to satisfy your competitive streak than allowing it to dominate at work, such as through sports or hobbies outside of the office environment.

Your strengths

It's the interview question we all expect: 'What are your greatest strengths?' You've probably reeled off your answer countless times, but I imagine that it's the answer you think you should give, not necessarily the one that's most true. That's because we don't always give it a great deal of thought.

It's vital, however, to identify and understand your personal and professional strengths, as they have a profound impact on both your performance and the overall success of your team. Research in the field of positive psychology emphasizes the importance of leveraging strengths to enhance motivation, engagement, and well-being.[2] By recognizing and utilizing your unique talents and abilities, you not only maximize your own potential but also inspire and empower your sales team to excel. Understanding your strengths allows you to allocate tasks strategically, creating a synergy between team members' individual proficiencies and organizational objectives. Moreover, leveraging strengths fosters a sense of fulfilment and energy, propelling you and your team toward exceptional achievements.

There are excellent tools you can use to discover your strengths, such as Gallup's CliftonStrengths Assessment[3] and the VIA Character Strengths Inventory.[4] They help you to gain a more objective view of what gives you an advantage, and you can use this knowledge to shape your views on what kind of leader you want to be. For instance, if you're brilliantly analytical and cool-headed in a crisis you'll be a different type of leader to one who leads from emotion, because you're you. That's as it should be.

A powerful tool I use with my coaching clients to help them identify their strengths is simply to get them to ask for feedback. Identify five people whom you trust and whose opinion you value. Then ask them these five questions:

1. What one word or phrase best describes me?

2. What do you think is my greatest achievement?

3. What do you value most about me?

4. What one thing could I change for my own benefit?

5. What do you believe is my greatest strength?

Research suggests that strengths can be continually enhanced, and new strengths can be developed with intentional effort and practice.[5] By acknowledging that our strengths are not fixed, we open ourselves up to continuous improvement and the opportunity to unleash our untapped potential. Embracing this mindset, we can shape our leadership style, leverage our unique abilities, and inspire others to thrive, fostering a culture of continuous growth and achievement.

Your motivations

We tend to enjoy doing what we're good at, so strengths and motivations often go hand in hand. Likewise, your list of top values will give you clues about what drives you to behave in certain ways.

You can also ask yourself these questions to learn more about your motivations.

1. What's the best day I've ever had at work, and why was it outstanding?

2. Conversely, when have I felt most demoralized?

3. Given the choice, how would I spend my day?

4. If time or money wasn't an issue, who would I help and how?

5. When I have a setback, how do I pick myself up afterwards?

Your answers will point you in the direction of what motivates you in your work. For instance, if your best day at work was when you took home the award for salesperson of the month, that says something different about your motivation than if it was when you worked out how to persuade a reluctant customer to stay with your business. Neither is right or wrong, they're just not the same.

When I was a sales leader myself, I'd often be asked for feedback by people who'd applied unsuccessfully for a management role. As I sat down with them and explored the reasons for applying for the position, it was usually because they simply saw management as the next step.

And yet when I looked at their values, strengths, and motivations, it was clear that it wasn't always what they truly wanted to do. It wasn't what they'd be good at or would make them happy. It's so important to understand these building blocks of your character because they determine what kind of leader you can best be, and even whether or not leadership is the right choice for you.

What's your why?

Understanding your values, strengths, and motivations is the starting point to knowing your 'why': the purpose behind what you do. At the risk of sounding tortuous, why do you need to know your why? Because it should define your purpose, and your purpose is the catalyst for the energy and effort you'll need to accomplish whatever you set out to do. It should be your desire, your reason, your core motivation – what drives you.

If you're familiar with the work of Simon Sinek, you'll know that he sees the 'why' as central to what makes a person or business unique.[6] It's always possible to copy *what* or *how* someone does something, but the *why* will always be untouchable. It's the result of a lifetime of experiences, thoughts, and ideas – the fingerprint of our actions.

Looking at leadership from the perspective of salespeople, rather than sales managers or leaders, there are far too many who dislike or are ambivalent about who they work for. That's because they've never gained any real value from them. Their leaders are focused on what they want for themselves, not on what their teams need from them. They don't have a purpose that's broader than themselves; they don't know their 'why.'

A conscious feeling of purpose is what many people have lost. Recently I carried out a training session with seven managers and leaders who were at different levels of their businesses, and when I asked them their 'why,' each of them gave an answer that was related to their performance level: 'I'm trying to hit my targets,' or 'I need to exceed my sales from the last quarter.' That's not a why, it's a goal. Your why goes far deeper than that.

Maslow's Hierarchy of Needs – a new take

You'll be familiar with Maslow's pyramid, and may reckon that you've heard everything there is to say about it. However, my take on it is a little different to what you might expect. I bring it in here because it helps you to understand how your 'why' fits into your work.

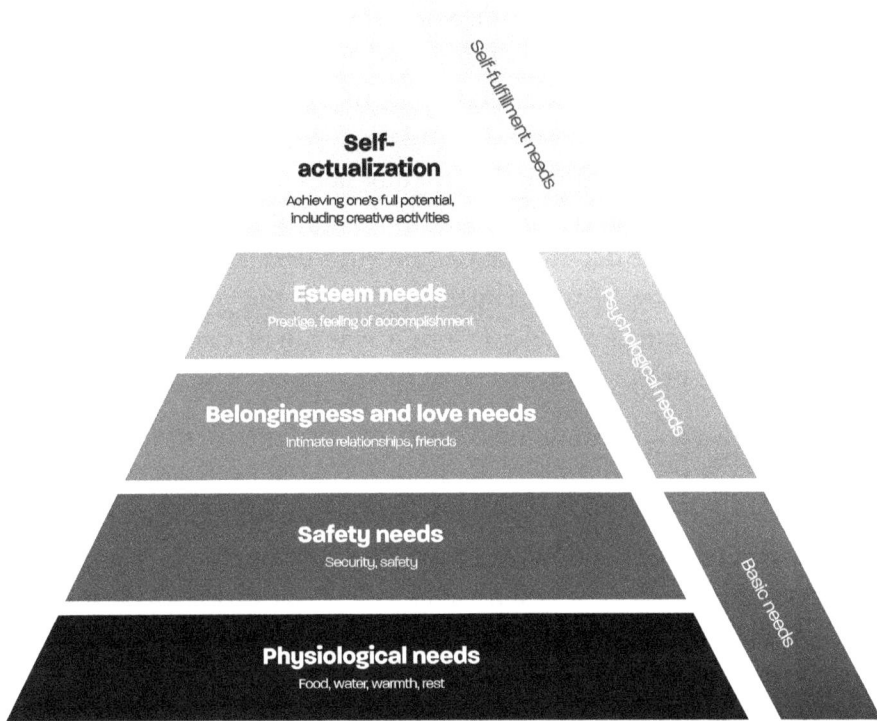

Self-actualization
Achieving one's full potential, including creative activities

Self-fulfillment needs

Esteem needs
Prestige, feeling of accomplishment

Belongingness and love needs
Intimate relationships, friends

Psychological needs

Safety needs
Security, safety

Physiological needs
Food, water, warmth, rest

Basic needs

At the bottom of the hierarchy sit our basic requirements for survival: physiological and safety needs. Once we've satisfied those we can move on to our belongingness and esteem needs, which help us to thrive and be happy; these relate to our relationships with others. At the top is self-actualization, or the realization of our talents and potential. This is what enables us to feel truly fulfilled.

It's the psychological needs in the middle that I'm interested in for now: esteem needs, and belongingness and love needs. Many people move into leadership positions to satisfy those needs. They crave the approval of their colleagues and fulfil their desire for status through the esteem in which they're held as a senior executive. However, you can't be a good leader if your motivation is based on those needs. Leadership is about realizing your potential, not bolstering your sense of emotional safety through your position. Certainly, self-esteem and a sense of belonging are important in any job, but they're not suitable for inspiring leadership.

It's important to understand this, because when your psychological needs are bound up in your role, you're vulnerable. You're looking to fulfil them in places that aren't designed for it. For instance, to satisfy your need for belonging you might play the role of your team's friend, when actually you're the boss. Or to satisfy your need for esteem you might focus disproportionately on your sales results, rather than on how you achieve them. You'll always be focusing on yourself, not your team, and will make decisions based on your best interests rather than on theirs and those of your organization. On the other hand, when you gain fulfilment as a leader through self-actualization, you can feel confident in your purpose.

Are you a leader because you want to earn more money or feel important? Or are you doing it because you want to make a difference and leave a valuable legacy? When you think about the leaders you've come across who've inspired you to deliver your best work, I hope that you'll see that it was the self-actualization level of the pyramid that they were operating from.

Your legacy

Cast your mind back to when you were first offered the job that you're in now. I expect, after a series of sweaty-palmed interviews and an anxious wait for the all-important phone call, you were over the moon when you heard the magic words: 'The job is yours.'

But imagine if, while you were still celebrating your success, I'd asked you the following questions: 'What's your exit plan from this job? And when will you know that it's time for you to leave?' What would you think? You'd probably feel as if I'd punctured your balloon. Why plan your resignation when you've barely got your feet under the table? And yet, there are sound reasons for doing this.

For a start, when you ask yourself these questions, you're challenging yourself to define what you want to achieve in your new role. What will success look like for you?

Take a moment to consider this, because you're far more likely to do a good job if you know the answer. You'll deal with multiple challenges every day, but when you know what you're aiming at in the long run it makes decision-making a lot easier. It gives you the confidence to know if you're doing the right things.

Second, the legacy you want to leave is integral to your success as a leader. What do you want people to say about you after you've gone? I hope it would be something along the lines of: *I'd love everyone who works for me to want to keep working for me, and I'd love everyone who manages me to want to retain me. That would show me that I've done a good job and have made a contribution that's worth something.*

Here are three questions to help you come up with a vision of your legacy.

1. How do you want to be remembered after you've left your current role?

2. What would you like to see in place in the future that's not there now?

3. Who and what would you like to have had an impact on, and in what way?

Now I'd like you to write down a vision of success for yourself. It's as if you're writing your own obituary, but for the job you're doing now rather than your own passing (let's not get too morbid). You could use the following format as a guide, filling in the blanks.

> *'Throughout my time in this role, I want to drive positive change in _____ by focusing on _____. Success for me means _____, and I want my leadership to be defined by _____.'*

Making yourself replaceable

By shifting your attention away from satisfying your psychological needs and towards realizing your potential, you're moving from being someone who fixes problems and manages resources to being a leader. Your focus is on developing people, rather than doing things for them. Eventually your team will be able to operate without you because they'll have the systems, skills, and confidence to do their jobs well. This is good for your organization because it's not dependent on you being around all the time; you've built an environment that's sustainable without you, which is what all good leaders do. In fact, one of the measures of a great leader is what happens when you are not around.

Does the thought of this make you feel a little insecure? What if you do such a good job of making yourself replaceable that your boss decides you're no longer needed? In my experience, this rarely happens. Being replaceable doesn't mean that you'll be fired or made redundant; on the contrary, you'll be viewed as someone who's created a high-growth team culture and a viable future for the business. Those above you will want to keep you and develop you, because you've become a prized commodity. You've created something bigger than yourself.

What's more, think about being replaceable from your boss's point of view. If you've spent your time being the only person who can solve every problem in your team, why would they want to support you with changing to a new or better role within your organization? The most likely scenario is that you'll find yourself stuck where you are.

The importance of confidence

When I talk to people in management positions, I often find that they feel insecure about their ability to lead. This is perfectly normal and is particularly the case if they're managing a team that they've recently been a member of; last week they were 'one of them,' and now they're supposed to be the boss. And yet confidence is key to successful leadership, because it enables you to be honest with yourself about your motivations, to make yourself replaceable, and to achieve extraordinary results.

To understand the importance of confidence, it's worth looking what happens when it's missing.

It stops you listening to what you don't want to hear

As organizational psychologist Adam Grant says, 'The thinner your skin, the thicker your skull becomes. A fragile ego leads you to deflect and attack: you're always in motion, but never changing. Feeling secure leads you to listen and learn: you can take one step back and move two steps forward.' In other words, when you feel insecure, you're always on the defensive. But when you feel confident, you're able to listen to constructive criticism.

It prevents you from improving things

Insecurity is the main reason for managers taking the credit for everything that goes well and dishing out the blame for what doesn't. Have you ever worked for someone like that? And were you inspired to do your best work for them?

It makes you unapproachable

Many leaders who are insecure compensate by adopting a macho approach. This creates an ultra-competitive environment in which people feel afraid to ask for help or to admit that they don't have all the answers. This has a toxic effect on their wellbeing and, just as importantly, on the performance of the team.

It makes you needy

Sometimes insecurity can drive a leader to feel as if they have to be popular; it's as if being wanted is more important to them than what they're trying to achieve for the business. There's nothing wrong with being liked and admired by your team – far from it. But if you're afraid to say anything that people might feel uncomfortable with, you'll find it difficult to make the right decisions.

It gives you false priorities

A false priority is one which says that we want something other than success. That sounds strange, but I'm sure you've encountered people who behave as if being right is more important than doing the right thing. This kind of thinking comes from insecurity, and ironically only reinforces it because it's impossible to feel confident when we operate from a position of fear and doubt.

In his book, *The Five Temptations of a CEO*, Patrick Lencioni describes a number of false priorities which can affect a manager or leader at any level, and work against achieving a high-growth culture.[7]

Choosing status over results. This is a natural but dangerous tendency to enjoy the position we have as a leader so much that we forget that our organization's success is more important.

Choosing popularity over accountability. This is when being liked is more important than confronting difficult decisions.

Choosing certainty over clarity. A leader needs clarity of purpose and has to feel comfortable with uncertainty.

Choosing harmony over conflict. This is when a leader thinks that consensus is always more important than challenging the status quo. Discomfort is the seeding ground for growing as individuals; if we stifle debate to keep everything nice, we'll never move beyond where we are now.

Choosing invulnerability over trust. Leadership expert John Maxwell tells a great story that illustrates the point that Lencioni is making here. A few years ago, Maxwell gave a talk to a group of leaders at a seminar. One of the points he made was that they should share their weaknesses with their people. This stimulated quite a reaction from the audience, and he sensed that there was resistance to the idea. Afterwards, one executive approached him and said that he appreciated most of what Maxwell had spoken about. But he had to disagree with the bit about leaders sharing their weaknesses. Surely leadership was about showing external confidence and never letting anyone see you sweat. How else would people feel inspired to follow you? John let him talk for a while, then interrupted. 'I think you're making a wrong assumption,' he said. 'You're assuming that your people don't already know your weaknesses. But they do. You're not telling them because they don't know, you're telling them so that they know you know. One of the most important things a leader can do is to accept reality. You can't lead other people effectively if you don't. In fact, you can't even lead yourself.

How to generate confidence

Of course, it's no good me saying: 'Be more confident.' When does that ever work? It's not as if you can conjure up confidence out of thin air. However, none of us were born feeling insecure – we learned it as we grew up. And if we learned it, we can unlearn it and replace it with its opposite. For most of us this takes a bit of work, but it's something that we can all achieve (and have fun with too). I'll focus first on two ways of countering a lack of confidence, and then on two ways of increasing it.

Understand the power of threat and reward

It's helpful to see where insecurity comes from. The NeuroLeadership Institute in New York, headed by David Rock, has developed a model that shows how lack of confidence is triggered in our brains. One of the themes that emerges is that much of the motivation driving social behaviour is governed by our desire to maximize reward and minimize threat. When conditions are good, we're relatively resourceful and engaged, feeling strong and happy. But when we're threatened, we retreat from the danger and focus our energies on minimizing the threat.

As an outcome from this research, Rock has developed his SCARF model, which identifies five domains of human social experience. These domains activate our brain's reward or threat circuitry, meaning that when we perceive a threat to our status, we actually interpret it in a similar way as a threat to our physical safety.

1. Status (relative importance to others)

2. Certainty (ability to predict the future)

3. Autonomy (how much control we have over events)

4. Relatedness (how safe we feel with others)

5. Fairness (our perception of fair exchanges between people)

This is strong stuff, but how does knowing it help us to feel more secure? We can't override our reactions to threats because they happen without our conscious input, but by knowing and labelling the responses we can rationally interpret them as what they are – primitive responses. For instance, if we know that when our boss criticizes us in front of our team, we're liable to react in a way that would make as much sense as if someone jumped us from behind, we're more likely to feel confident in acting with dignity instead of starting a petty argument.

It's particularly worth focusing on the domain of certainty because, in most leadership positions, the higher up the chain of command you are the less of it you have. Problems arise to which you don't have the answers, and nor do you necessarily have anyone to ask for help. Unlike when you were a salesperson, your certainty now has to come from your 'why' – your purpose. This helps to give you clarity and motivation, which makes that uncomfortable feeling of not being sure what to do much easier to manage.

De-clutter the noise

I sometimes wish that I could make a recording of what goes on inside the average brain, because my guess is that there's a heck of a lot of noise in there. False assumptions are one such area of noise: the kind of thinking that's not based on reality and therefore can't be tested. *I'm terrible at presentations – if only I was as good as x*, or *I'll never be respected by the other members of the board*. One way of looking at this is to ask yourself if your belief would stand up in a court of law. Is there sufficient evidence to support it? I imagine a half decent barrister would demolish your argument pretty quickly.

You can also tackle false assumptions by applying some common sense. When I talk to someone who's feeling unsure and anxious about something, I often say, 'Well, what's the worst that could happen? Let's try to imagine. Could you deal with it?' The answer is invariably 'Yes,' because we can solve any problem if we have to. Next, I ask, 'And how likely is it that it would actually happen?' The answer is, of course, 'Not likely.' You can try this for yourself by imagining your worst-case scenario and listing all the things you would do to cope with it if it came about. I'm confident that you could come up with several. And that's the very worst-case situation – the reality will probably be far less challenging.

Another type of false thinking is when we generalize, talking in terms of 'everyone' and 'always.' Here we're confusing opinions with facts, assuming that because something has happened once it will recur in the future. We tend to do this when we feel negative, which generates another batch of noise: that of automatically seeing the downside in things. It's hard to feel confident enough to try something new when you're in the habit of judging your experiences so harshly.

Why is it that we generate this internal noise? It's because of the mental shortcuts that we've created over the years to make life more predictable for ourselves. In the ancient past these might have helped us to survive, but in today's business environment they can slowly sap our confidence and enthusiasm. What was once useful (*That looks like a lion. A lion once ate my brother. I need to avoid the lion.*) is now a ball and chain. Just like with the SCARF model, when we know what's going on it makes it a lot easier to rationalize the unhelpful thoughts. Through understanding that they're shortcuts, we only need to take one further step to realize that they serve no useful function in a leadership role.

The 'be, do, get' formula

Suppose I want to lose weight – that's what I want to 'get.' So, I go on a diet and increase my gym visits to five times a week – that's what I 'do.' But as so often sadly happens, my high-minded ambitions fade away after a month and gradually I slip back into my old ways. Why is this? It's because I didn't pay attention to the 'be' part of the equation – the bit that's about my mindset and beliefs. I didn't see myself as someone who eats healthily and exercises regularly, but as someone who was trying to do those things.

It is crucial to cultivate a clear perception of the desired outcomes we strive to attain. Maxwell Maltz, a pioneering researcher and author, introduced the concept of Psycho-Cybernetics, highlighting the power of the mind to focus, direct, and recalibrate its efforts until it reaches the intended goal.[8] Maltz's groundbreaking work emphasized the profound influence of self-image, a term he popularized, on an individual's ability to succeed or falter in achieving their goals. He also introduced effective techniques such as visualization, mental rehearsal, and relaxation to enhance and manage one's self-image.

When we believe we're already something, it gives us the confidence to be it in reality. And then, once we've believed it for a while and started doing it, we get the results we're looking for and our faith in ourselves is enhanced. It's the same with leadership. If we think, 'I'm a leader,' rather than, 'I'm doing leadership things,' we create a mental image of ourselves as a leader. This is all the easier to do when we know what kind of leader we want to be and why.

I find that the key thing with creating a vision for yourself is to set it in the present tense. So not, *I'll be a great leader in five years' time*, but *I'm a leader now, and I'm getting better as each month goes by*. 'Be' it before you 'do' it, and you're much more likely to 'get' it. It's a trick of the mind.

Pay attention to your emotions

There's a general belief that emotions don't belong at work. However, there's no sense in this because – as we know – many people feel insecure, and insecurity is a feeling. We humans are emotional creatures, and when problems arise it's natural to feel stressed, disappointed, or angry. This can lead us to doubt ourselves even more. Not only has something bad happened, but we're overcome with negative feelings about it as well.

Part of developing confidence is accepting our emotions, but also nurturing ways of managing them. We should understand the impact they have, but also that it's not a good idea to let them take control of us. When this happens, we're likely to say things we regret, make knee-jerk decisions out of stress, and generally behave in a non-leader-like way. The good news is that when you know what your values are and what you're wanting to achieve in your role, it helps you to feel grounded. And feeling grounded is one of the best ways I know of feeling secure. It's a virtuous circle.

Looking after yourself

This leads me to the various ways in which you can look after your emotional wellbeing. I'm sure that you have your tried and tested methods for picking yourself up after a bad day or calming yourself down when you're in the middle of a stressful meeting. The processes I'm about to describe here aren't designed to replace them but to give you some alternative ideas, especially if what you're already doing isn't helping that much.

Journaling

This is simply the process of writing down your thoughts. Calling it 'journaling' makes it sound a little formal, but you don't need a special book or anything fancy to do it with – a scrap of paper or your phone will do. The reason I recommend it is because it enables you to organize and clarify what's in your head, which in turn helps you to handle your emotions and deal with your insecurities. There's nothing like writing down your thoughts and feelings to help you to reflect, analyze, and work them through.

What's more, journaling is private. It's a way of communicating your highs and lows in a way that no-one else will see. You could think of it as a safe space to offload without worrying about someone judging you for it.

You can also use journaling for other reasons, such as goal setting, generating creative ideas, and reinforcing enjoyable memories and experiences. When you write something down, you're telling your brain that it's important, so your intentions for your next sales target or your musings on how to deal with a difficult person will take on a new meaning. It's worth giving it a go.

Practising mindfulness

One thing that stops people becoming great leaders is stress and overwhelm, which is where mindfulness can help. It involves focusing purely on the present moment: the room you're in, the chair you're sitting on, your breathing, your current activity. There have been many studies carried out that show the neurological impact of mindfulness in terms of its ability to help us think more clearly.[9] This in turn aids decision-making. There are whole books written on mindfulness, so I won't go into detail here, but if you're interested in taking it further a good place to start is *Mindfulness for Dummies*.[10]

Working with a coach or mentor

As Eric Schmidt, ex-CEO of Google, said, 'The one thing that people are never good at is seeing themselves as others see them. A coach really, really helps.' This gets to the heart of how a coach can help you to develop yourself as a leader, as well as giving you the tools to increase your self-confidence. Their role is to hold a mirror up to you and reflect what's really there. It's not necessarily a comfortable process, but a good coach will support you as you grow with them. I've seen countless people transform themselves from being insecure, confused, and directionless to feeling confident in their purpose – all through coaching.

Alternatively (or additionally) you can work with a mentor. There's a quote that I love about the distinction between a coach and a mentor: 'A coach has some great questions for your answers; a mentor has some great answers for your questions.' A coach isn't necessarily an expert in your field; their role is to draw out the inner leader from within you. A mentor is someone who has either done something that you want to do or has a skill or way of doing it that you want to develop in yourself. In fact, you can have several mentors if you like, each helping you with different elements of your role.

To find the right mentor you need to be clear on what you want to develop, whether it be a skill or a career ambition. For instance, you might feel the need to improve your financial planning skills so that you can generate better forecasts and profit analyzes. Or you could aspire to move up to the next level of leadership and want someone who's already there to advise you on how to do it. Your first step is to identify someone who not only has the credentials you're looking for but is someone you could get on with. They don't have to work in your own company or even in sales, nor do they need to be more senior than you. They just need to be someone you admire, and who's achieved the thing you want to achieve.

After you've gained their agreement to spend a little time with you, you can ask them some pre-prepared questions. Here are a few ideas for ones that will draw out the most insightful responses.

- What do you think is my biggest strength or weakness in this area?

- What are the five things that have given you the most success?

- Can you break down how you became good at each one?

- Can you teach me/watch me do it/give me feedback/help me with this?

Mentoring doesn't have to be a formal affair. You don't necessarily need to ask someone if they'll be your mentor – it could be a chat over coffee or a series of casual meetings. It might even be that you get to know someone in your office who seems good at something, and slowly a mentoring-like relationship evolves. All that matters is that you're seeking to learn from them.

I guarantee that some of the most successful leaders you know have worked with coaches and mentors for much of their careers. They might use different terminology for them and there may be some overlap in terms of the support they provide, but essentially that's what they are. It's a myth that anyone is a born leader who can succeed without help and advice. You become a great leader by doing the right things well, and you can't do this unless you know who you are. A coach or mentor can help you to see that, and this in turn gives you confidence, courage, and clarity of purpose. That's the basis of a high-growth mentality.

In the next chapter we'll start looking at how you can put leadership into action, including the all-important element of managing your time.

Key takeaways

- Effective leadership starts with self-awareness – understanding your values, strengths, and motivations to define your style and 'why.'

- Begin your leadership role with a clear vision of the legacy you want to leave, guiding long-term decisions and actions.

- Confidence is essential for leadership and can be built through self-reflection, managing insecurities, and embracing growth.

- Support systems, such as coaching, mentorship, and mindfulness practices, help leaders navigate challenges and sustain their effectiveness.

- Aligning personal purpose with professional actions fosters trust, credibility, and a high-growth leadership culture.

PART 2

YOUR TEAM

You've now spent some time exploring yourself as a leader – how you think, how you react, and how you show up under pressure. That's the foundation of great sales leadership. But being self-aware isn't enough. Your next challenge is to translate that growth into how you lead others. This next part of the book is all about *your team* – how you guide, support, and develop them to perform at their best.

Now that you understand where your problems lie, it's time to explore solutions. In this part of the book, you'll discover ways of liberating your time so that you have the space to implement new working methods and transformational ways of motivating and developing your people. By the end, you'll have a toolkit for positive change.

Chapter 5

When do I find time for all this?

At a recent leadership workshop for a group of sales managers, I shared many of the ideas that I've spoken about so far. They included the fact that to become effective leaders they should make their main focus the development of their teams. We explored what this would mean for each of them, and they gave me a piece of feedback that I find to be the most common whenever I lead sessions like this. It goes as follows:

> *This all sounds great – but only in an ideal world. If I had more time/if I had a boss who understood how important personal development was/ if the other people I work with weren't so disorganized, I could easily see myself leading from the front rather than running around in circles like I am now. But my situation is different. I simply don't have the hours in the day to train and develop people – it's all I can do to keep the show on the road as it is. Nice idea, but it won't work for me.*

I get it – I really do. But this objection comes from asking the wrong question. Instead of it being, *When do I fit being a leader into my day?* it should be, *When do I fit everything else around being a leader?* Because if you want to create a high-growth team and achieve amazing results, inspiring and developing your people isn't an optional extra. It's central to everything you do.

Okay, so it's a matter of priorities. But that still doesn't help me magic up the time I need. If I put training and development front and centre it will just mean that other stuff won't get done, and that's important too.

I get that as well, which is why this chapter will show you how to see your time in an entirely different way than you may be used to.

The three roles of the sales leader

Over the years I've come to see sales leaders as having three distinct roles. How well you perform in your job depends on how you carry out these roles. They are:

1. the customer leader;

2. the business leader; and

3. the people leader.

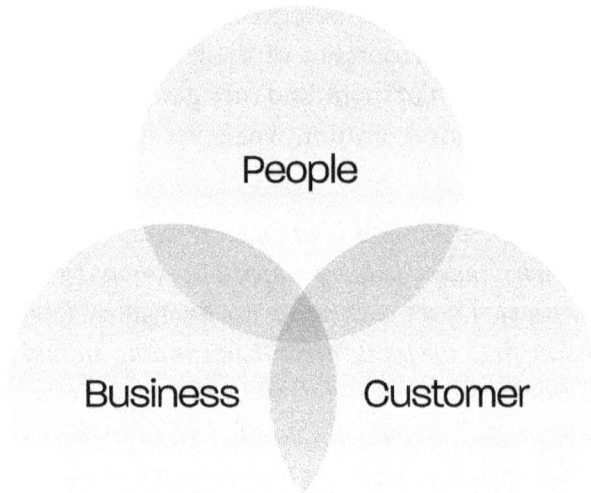

The customer leader

Many sales managers still assume some responsibility for selling, even if it only takes the form of supporting their people at important customer meetings. Most have also been salespeople in the past – often highly successful ones – and they can't resist the thrill of the chase when it comes to bagging a big deal. It's in their blood. They love this aspect of their jobs and are often keen to expend a lot of time and energy on it. And why not? It helps to rack up the all-important numbers. However, this focus on closing deals for salespeople, rather than coaching them to do it themselves, is what I referred to in Chapter 3 as being deal managers rather than sales leader. It doesn't help their teams to develop, or themselves to become better leaders.

The business leader

This role is about the organizational aspects of the job: reporting, forecasting, planning, monitoring progress, and other administrative tasks. While few sales managers enjoy this area, it's one that they often spend time in because they have to. When senior management demands a report, they're obliged to deliver it. This is why, while some of these tasks are important, they can still take up far too much of a sales manager's time.

The people leader

This is the most important role for sales managers, although it's also the one that's most neglected. It's to do with coaching and supporting their teams. In other words, not doing people's jobs for them or being absent while busy with paperwork, but helping them to grow. It's about building their capacity and enabling them to achieve their objectives.

Have a think about how much time you spend in each of these three areas. What would it amount to over the average week and month? If you find yourself without enough time for your people role, it's probably because you're spending too much of it in one or both of the others. In future chapters you'll learn ways of combining these roles more holistically, so that people development becomes embedded into the way you carry out your business and customer roles. This will help you to get more done in your day. But for now, this is a starting point to help you see how unbalanced your day-to-day activities may have become.

A life lesson

I love this story, because no matter how many times I tell it I gain a new insight. Even if you've heard it before, please still give it a read as it will mean something different to you now that you've thought about your three roles.

A philosophy professor found himself on the receiving end of repeated complaints from his students about their workloads. How were they supposed to finish their dissertations when they had so many lectures to attend and assignments to complete? He decided to give them a life lesson. One day, as they filed into the lecture theatre, they were surprised to see a large glass jar on the table at the front. 'This,' the professor explained, 'represents the time that each of you has available – the number of hours in the day.'

The students sat down, intrigued. The professor then reached below the table and pulled out four or five big rocks, dropping them into the jar until they reached the top. 'Is the jar full?' he asked. Most of the students nodded but one said, 'No. There are some gaps between the rocks.' The professor replied, 'You're absolutely right.' He reached down and retrieved a small sack of pebbles, pouring them into the jar and shaking them around the rocks until they settled between them.

'Now,' he asked. 'Is the jar full?' Again, most of the students agreed that it was, apart from the same student who had dissented before. 'No. You can see there are gaps between the pebbles, even if they're really small.' The professor nodded: 'You're right.' (At this point I start to imagine the rest of the class shifting with irritation – who was this smart Alec?). He reached under the table and brought out a bag of sand, decanting it into the jar between the rocks and pebbles. Then he asked again: 'Is it full?' Even the student who'd disagreed before nodded this time.

The professor explained that the filled jar was a metaphor for life. We each of us have our own jar, which represents the 24 hours available in a day, and the question isn't how much time we have but how we use it. 'The big rocks are your priorities,' he said. In this particular case he was talking about the most important things in our lives such as our family and health. The pebbles, he went on to explain, were less important things, such as jobs and cars. And the sand represented the small stuff. If the students spent all their time and energy on this, they'd never have time for what mattered most to them. They needed to take care of their rocks first and ensure that everything else fitted around them.

At this moment a voice piped up from the back of the room: 'Actually, the jar's still not full.' All heads swivelled around to see a different student, this time with unruly hair and dirty trainers. Even the professor looked surprised. The student walked to the front, reached into his backpack, and brought out a can of beer. With a deft movement he cracked open the can and poured the liquid into the jar, watching it run between the pebbles and soak into the sand. 'Why did you do that?' asked the professor. 'Because there's always time for a beer,' said the student.

I admit I made up the last bit about the beer. But being serious, this fable illustrates that the concept of time management is a fallacy. You can't manage time; you can only manage what you do within the time you have available. As a leader, your people development represents one of your big rocks. You need to schedule time with them so that your people role isn't squeezed out of the way the minute a tricky customer starts complaining or the latest sales report is due. Imagine if, at the start of each month or quarter, you were to plan in your 'people rocks' and ensure that everything else fitted around them. How would that change your outlook on the way you spend your time?

Take this opportunity to list your three biggest rocks as they are today:

1. _____

2. _____

3. _____

Being honest, are they the right ones? Or could you replace them with more important rocks? And if you find it hard to work out what's most important, read on.

Urgent versus important

The concept of prioritization is hopefully clear for you, but you may be wondering how you're going to downgrade some tasks while upgrading others. What should rise up the list and what should sink to the bottom, or drop off altogether? The key to this is having an in-depth understanding of what's *important* to you, as opposed to what's *urgent*.

The interplay between urgent and important is often shown on a grid known as the Eisenhower Matrix. President Eisenhower constantly had to make difficult decisions about which tasks he should focus on each day, once saying 'I have two kinds of problems, the urgent and the important. The urgent are not important, and the important are never urgent.' This dilemma led him to develop the Eisenhower principle and his approach to how he organized his workload and priorities. This has been developed into a framework, and it helps us to choose what to focus on.

Urgent / Important

- Customer complaints or escalations
- Team crises needing immediate action
- Critical deadlines
- Preventable problems now urgent

Not urgent / Important

- Coaching and developing people
- Planning and preparation
- Building key relationships
- Spotting problems early
- Improving how things work

Urgent / Not important

- Doing others work for them
- Last-minute reporting/admin
- Unnecessary calls and meetings
- 'Urgent' emails that aren't
- Solving instead of coaching

Not urgent / Not important

- Inbox tidying and busywork
- Rearranging files or systems
- Endless scrolling or Slack checking
- Office gossip and politics
- Tasks that look busy but aren't

The most common interpretation of this tool is that we should always focus first on quadrant 1, or urgent and important tasks. However, my take on it is different. Urgent and important is another way of describing what's more commonly known as firefighting, and it usually consists of things that have become urgent because we've not dealt with them properly in the first place. When we operate in this space, we feel overwhelmed. We rush around dealing with one emergency after another, clearing up the mess that we (or others) have left behind from previous problems. This is when we put in place sticking plaster solutions, such as doing people's jobs for them rather than helping them to learn for themselves. After a day of this, when we're collapsed in an exhausted heap, we vow we'll never let it happen again. But somehow, we always do.

It's far more productive to focus your time and energy on quadrant 2, or non-urgent and important tasks. This is the quadrant in which you plan, prepare, schedule, and think things through. It's also where your development of your team takes place. After all, a professional firefighter only spends a small proportion of their week extinguishing flames; most of it is taken up with prevention work that minimizes the likelihood of emergencies arising in the first place. Every hour that you spend here is magnified in its effects later on, when you reap the rewards of your forward thinking.

Quadrant 3, or urgent and not important, is an interesting one. It consists of tasks I like to call OPC (or Other People's Crap). When a last-minute crisis lands on our desks, it fires up our adrenaline and we can become seduced into thinking it's vital to deal with, even if it's not. We assume that we're being productive by solving it quickly, but we're actually just being busy. When we're productive we're moving forwards, but when we're busy we're running around in circles. We've become used to saying, 'I'm so busy' as if it's a badge of honour, but how about if we said, 'I'm so productive'? It doesn't sound as catchy but at least we'd know we were achieving something worthwhile. In some ways being busy is a form of laziness, because it involves doing things without thinking about whether they're important.

Quadrant 4, or non-urgent and not important, could be described as escapism. It's where we procrastinate by tidying up our computer desktops, or getting sucked into office politics instead of doing something more constructive with our time. There's nothing wrong with a bit of escapism – we all need to decompress every now and then – but ideally it should be treated as a big rock and scheduled in, much like a vacation.

When we think we're 'too busy' to take time off, we let our stress levels build up; this leads us to resort to unhealthy methods of escape, and it becomes a vicious circle.

Think of elite athletes. They love competing, but they know they can't do it all the time, or they'll become ineffectual. Rest and recuperation are part of their training system, and so it should be with us.

What do we mean by 'urgent' and 'important'?

It's worth thinking about what we mean by these words, because they've become misused over the years. 'Urgent' is pretty obvious, in that it's when something has an imminent deadline attached to it requiring immediate attention or action. If I schedule my Christmas shopping for November (which I always intend to do, but never get around to), it's not urgent. It's important, but it only becomes urgent if it's Christmas Eve and I still haven't done it.

'Important' is more interesting. What defines something as being important? How do you decide? There are four questions you can ask yourself about a task.

1. **Does it align with my objectives and goals?** If you're clear about what you want to achieve in your role, then any activity that you invest time in should ideally contribute towards it. An example for me is time with my family. Everything I do revolves around my kids, which means that having space in my day for them is extremely important to me. I therefore never schedule any business trips during the school holidays. I can still choose to work then if I want to, but my starting point is that I book the time off and this helps me to achieve my goal and, importantly, is aligned with my values.

2. **Does it move me forwards?** An important activity should always do this. Firefighting, by definition, only takes you back to where you started because you've solved the immediate problem

but haven't put in place any long-term solution. Important work is that which takes you to a more advanced place than you were before. Look at what you actually gain by doing this work.

3. **What would happen if I didn't do it?** It's clearly helpful to know what consequences there could be if you didn't do a task. Sometimes they'll be serious, in which case the activity must be important. But at other times, if you're honest, there would be few major issues if you let it go, and you could therefore categorize it as unimportant. This distinction might not be obvious at first glance, especially if the task is also urgent, so it's worth thinking through.

4. **Am I really the best person to do this?** It could be that the activity on the whole is important but is it really your responsibility to complete it. I don't mean this is some sort of 'not my job' type defiance, rather is there someone better placed and more suited to complete the activity. Is it actually someone else's responsibility or could the task be delegated?

What can you do to make sure that you make the best use of your time? Time which should mainly be spent developing your team, rather than selling or writing reports? The causes of your overwhelm, dissatisfaction, and frustration are almost always due to you spending it in the wrong areas of the matrix. The solution is to avoid quadrants 3 and 4, which are filled with tasks that are unimportant; carefully manage how much time you spend in quadrant 1, which is filled with urgent obligations; and focus as much as possible on quadrant 2, the non-urgent and important area.

Quadrant 2 is where the magic lies. The more time you spend there, the better prepared you'll be to face any challenge. You'll find yourself

▷ empowering your people to improve how they work so they're less likely to need your help;

▷ warding off crises by planning and preparing your tasks properly;

▷ avoiding having to re-do your work by getting it right first time; and

▷ enjoying your job because you feel in control.

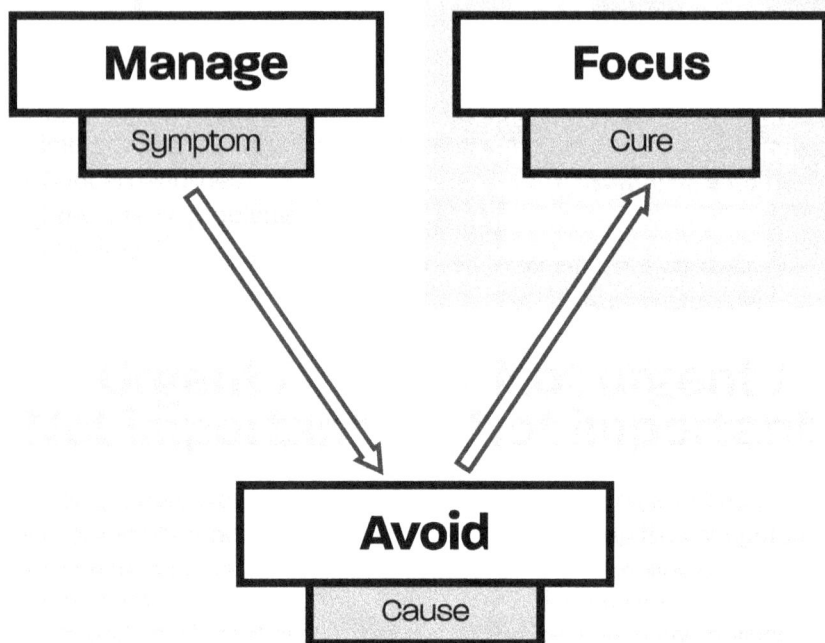

Of course, you can't prevent every emergency – there will always be times when the unexpected happens. But by ensuring that the majority of your work is scheduled in, you can drastically reduce the number of fires you have to put out. And a lack of firefighting makes for a productive and inspiring leader.

Yeah but...

> This sounds great in theory, but I have a boss who's always telling me they want things done by the end of the day. There's no way I can avoid those urgent quadrants – it won't work for me.

I'm often challenged to respond to this objection, and if this relates to you there are some ways you can deal with the problem. One is that you can carry on the way you are, but I'm guessing that's not what you really want. Another is that you can look at what you can control, rather than what you can't. Could you explain to your boss the effect it has on your ability to be productive? Can you show them how you're now organizing your time, so they can see the impact of dumping their crises onto you? The more organized you are, the better position you'll be in to highlight what you won't be able to accomplish if you deal with their problem today.

> *I've tried that, but my boss still won't listen. He has no idea about planning and thinking ahead.*

So, the option above might not work for you. But what about this one? What if you were to schedule one hour each day for dealing with your manager's emergencies? If you don't need it, you have that hour back, but if you do, you can put out the fire and still cover your own priorities.

I understand why people object to changing their way of working, because we'd all love the silver bullet – the brilliant result that doesn't require us to do anything differently. However, we have choices in how we work, even if we think we don't. When you're a leader, you shouldn't be dealing with emergences on a regular basis, nor should you be fixing people's problems for them. The vast majority of what you do can be planned and scheduled. When this is done, you're able to deal calmly with unexpected situations because you know that the vital work is taken care of. And just as importantly, you come across as the influential leader you want to be – one who's in control.

The brakes on a car

Ben Feldman was one of the most successful salespeople in US history; by 1979 he'd sold more life insurance than anyone else, at a total value of $1.5 billion. He famously said: 'Sales isn't a problem, it's a process. And when it ceases to be a process, it's a problem.'

There's a close relationship between operating in quadrant 2 (non-urgent and important tasks), and systems and processes. Some people roll their eyes at the thought of processes because they assume they're constraining and cumbersome, but to this I say: 'What are the brakes on a car for?' Most reply that they're to slow the car down. But they're not, they're actually to allow it to go faster. Because the better the brakes, the faster the car is capable of travelling safely. In the same way, systems and processes (if they're good ones) enable you to move more quickly and perform at a higher level than if you don't have them.

So how does this work? What are the advantages of systems and processes?

They enable you to improve

When you do things in a consistent way, you're able to improve on them because you can identify what's working and what's not. Take a tennis player, for instance. One of the first things their coach does is to analyze what they consistently do well and badly, so that they can build on that. If the player is completely random in their game it will be almost impossible for the coach to help them improve.

Or take another example, this time from manufacturing. Suppose you own a car factory and are shocked to see a sharp rise in quality problems. You ask the foreman what's going on and he says, 'We decided to abandon our processes and build the cars however we liked – it's more fun that way. Sure, the systems we had before worked well, but we fancied a change.' I can imagine what you would think.

And if you assume that systems are fine for objects but not for people, consider the healthcare industry. Surgeons have checklists to ensure that nothing is overlooked when they carry out an operation, and GPs use processes to refer patients for specialist treatment so that the overall system works in a coherent way. Systems and processes create a consistent environment in which flaws and areas for improvement can be more easily spotted than when things are done randomly.

They help to prevent crises

When you work within a process, you're able to spot a problem coming over the horizon, because by definition a crisis is a deviation from the norm. This enables you to deal with it ahead of time, before it takes over your day. You also have the breathing space to put in place a more permanent fix, so that the issue is less likely to arise again.

They make life easier

Systems free up mental space for you, because you're not making things up as you go along. When you've designed a process that's geared towards you achieving your goals, and follow it, you're not having to decide afresh each time how to go about it. You can now cash in that energy surplus and spend it in other areas that might need your attention.

Despite the concrete benefits of creating and working with great systems and processes, many sales managers don't give themselves the benefit of them. They do their own thing, whether it be for selling, recruiting, training, or any other aspect of their jobs. This leads to a haphazard approach in which they're constantly thinking on the fly, spending time on whatever seems most urgent. It's a great shame, because they could be making their lives a lot easier if they had processes to follow.

Monkey see, monkey do

Scientists in the 1960s conducted a series of experiments into learned behaviour. The basis of this research was to see if the behaviour of one subject (in this case a rhesus monkey) could create a lasting effect on another one. For their study, the scientists placed five rhesus monkeys in a large cage. Positioned in the middle was a stepladder and, just within reach at the top of the cage, was a bunch of ripe bananas. Whenever a monkey attempted to climb the ladder and get to the bananas, *all* the monkeys would be blasted with freezing cold water. Eventually the monkeys gave up going for the bananas, because they'd learned to associate the punishment of the freezing water with their attempts to grab the fruit.

Here's where it became interesting. The scientists then removed one of the monkeys and replaced it with a new one, which immediately tried to retrieve the bananas. Instead of being sprayed with water, it was set upon by the rest of the group, who pulled it off the ladder and beat it. After several beatings the new monkey also learned not to go after the bananas, even though it didn't know why.

A second monkey from the original group was then substituted and the same thing happened. All the monkeys beat the newcomer when it went for the bananas, including the monkey that had never been drenched by the water. As this new monkey learned not to try and reach the fruit, a third monkey was replaced, and the same behaviour was repeated. The scientists swapped out a fourth monkey, and eventually the fifth and final monkey from the original group was changed.

None of the remaining monkeys had ever been blasted with freezing water, and yet they still didn't attempt to reach the bananas. In fact, they continued to beat up and prevent any new monkeys from climbing the ladder.[1]

So, what does this story have to do with systems and processes? It's not possible to ask the monkeys why they behaved the way they did. If they were able to talk, I guess their reply would go something along the lines of, 'It's always been like this', or 'It's just how things are done around here.' In other words, processes can take on a life of their own. What might have been the right way of doing things at one time, in response to certain events, may not be true today. We continue to behave in a particular way but have long since forgotten why. If you're new to the role of sales manager, it's all too easy to pick up from where your predecessor left off – running the same meetings, producing the same reports, and following the same processes – because it's just how things are done around here.

These systems have a deep impact on your team's culture. As a leader, part of your responsibility is to establish rules for others to follow. You're the research scientist, not the monkey. So, while it's important to acknowledge the value of processes, you should also ask how many of them are still relevant and whether they can be improved. Left unchecked, outdated systems create accepted norms that get in the way of growth and innovation. They stop you and your team learning and seeing things from different perspectives. And they can also waste everyone's time, as is often the case, for instance, with meetings which don't have a clear objective or where the attendees don't have an agenda to follow.

I suggest that you carry out a simple audit of your systems and processes as they exist today, such as meetings, reports, and other regular activities. Have you got caught up in ways of doing things that are now past their sell-by date? Or do they help you and your team to move towards your goals? This is quadrant 2 thinking – preventing problems and planning how to accomplish tasks well, rather than waiting until something goes wrong and fixing it.

There's an interesting piece of research which explores the effect a manager has on their people. The study looked at what a manager pays attention to, measures, rewards, and controls, and the behaviours a manager displays themselves. The results reveal that 80 to 90% of a person's behaviour is influenced by their manager.[2] For instance, if a manager focuses heavily on cost saving, their team will too; and if the manager is constantly in crisis mode, their people will see firefighting as the accepted way of doing things. This shows how much of what your people do is within your control – your approach is critical for the way they do their jobs. Your systems and processes are a core part of 'how we do things around here', so it's worth making sure that they're fit for purpose.

Having read this chapter, you might be feeling that it leaves you with more questions than answers. That's a good thing, because it shows you're starting to challenge some long-held habits and assumptions, and it's not an uncommon response when I teach this topic to groups. I'm assuming that you're reading this book because you want something to change, and it follows that if you want different results you need to do some things differently. That can be a challenge, and you'll find the answers to your questions coming to you more and more as you evolve as a leader.

Now that you understand the value of using your time effectively, you're well placed to move onto the next chapter, in which we look at how to create an engaged and energized sales team.

Key takeaways

- ▷ Leadership is the core of your role, and developing your team should be your top priority.

- ▷ Effective time management means focusing on high-value tasks that drive growth, especially team development.

▷ Prioritize non-urgent but important tasks, reduce time spent on urgent activities, and eliminate unimportant distractions.

▷ Systems and processes act as enablers, allowing consistent performance and minimizing crises.

▷ A proactive approach to time and task management fosters a high-growth team culture and long-term success.

Chapter 6
Keys to building an engaged team

You know how there are some leaders who have teams that seem to do everything right? Their people are enthusiastic and motivated, they enjoy their jobs, and they get brilliant results. These teams are few and far between, but I imagine you've seen one or two in your time. Maybe you're even lucky enough to have been a member of one.

How do those leaders do it? What's the magic formula? Are they just lucky with the people they lead, or is there something else to it? And if so, what?

The truth is that almost anyone can be an inspirational and engaging leader. There's no dark art involved, you don't have to be born with innate charisma (whatever that means), and you certainly don't need to be blessed with the 'right' kind of people in your team for it to work. In this chapter, we'll explore the nuts and bolts of how to engage, energize, and mobilize your team, so that you can fulfil the all-important 'people' part of your role. This is the crux of what it means to be a great leader.

How engaged is your team?

You may have heard the term 'employee engagement' a few times in your career. But what is it and why does it matter?

There are many ways of defining engagement, but the one I like the best is from HR consultancy Mercer: 'A state of mind in which employees feel a vested interest in the company's success and are both willing and motivated to perform to levels that exceed the stated job requirements. It is the result of how employees feel about the work experience – the organization, its leaders, the work, and the work environment.'[1] You'll notice the emphasis on words describing emotions: 'feel', 'willing', and 'motivated'. Being engaged isn't a rational, logical act – it's a response that comes from deeper within. Nor is it the same as being satisfied at work or enjoying one's job; these are good things, but they're the result of a one-way process. They give to the employee, but they don't necessarily reap a similar amount for the employer.

The benefits of having an engaged team

The top-line benefit of leading an engaged team is that your people give you a higher level of discretionary effort. They work harder for you, and are more loyal to you, than if they were disengaged. This has a concrete impact on your sales.

In 2009, The Institute for Employment Studies (IES) published a comprehensive piece of research which explored what engagement is and how it can be achieved.[2] I'm particularly struck with this point: 'Employee engagement is a hard-nosed proposition that not only shows results but can be measured in costs of recruitment and employee output.'[3] In other words, there's a solid financial reason for engaging people – it's not just some fluffy ideal.

Let's look at the benefits of having an engaged team in more detail.[4]

> **Customer loyalty.** The research shows that people who are engaged with their work tend to have a good understanding of how to meet customer needs, which increases customer loyalty. They can even generate twice as many repeat purchases as disengaged employees.

- **Employee retention.** A total of 41% of engaged employees say that they'd stay with their organization even if it was struggling to survive. Engagement is positively related to a commitment to the business, which reduces recruitment and onboarding costs.

- **Productivity.** When people feel engaged, they're likely to go the extra mile, perform at higher levels, take the initiative when needed, and be enthusiastic about learning for themselves. This makes the team they work within more efficient and productive.

- **Advocacy of the organization.** Engaged employees tend to recommend their organization to potential employees and customers, whereas disengaged ones do the opposite. In other words, engagement makes it easier for you to recruit more customers and salespeople.

- **Manager success.** People who are engaged tend to respond positively to their managers. This helps those managers do a better job of leading them, creating a virtuous circle of productive relationships.

- **Bottom-line profit.** This is the result of various aspects of having engaged employees, such as increased productivity, customer loyalty, higher sales, and better staff retention levels. For instance, a study of 2,000 UK banks found that with every 10% rise in engagement levels came a 4% increase in sales.

This sounds great, and yet few people are truly engaged with their work. In Gallup's 2017 State of the American Workplace report, 67% of employees are either not engaged or are actively disengaged.[5] The disengaged group is looking for other jobs, and even behaving in a way that's detrimental to the organization. This costs the company in staff attrition and poor performance, and it costs leaders in the amount of effort they have to put in to keep people motivated.

Given that the upside of having an engaged team is so high, and the downside so low, our next question should be: what does it take to create one? This is what we'll go on to explore, but key to it is your influence as a manager. The IES research is clear that managers are essential for recruiting people who are committed to doing quality work. Once they're in, it's the quality of the relationship they have with those people that can be the crucial driver of engagement. 'Leaders and managers who inspire confidence in individuals, giving them autonomy to make decisions with clear goals and accountability, are perceived as engaging… The actions and integrity of leaders and line managers are vitally important in enabling engagement.'[6] In other words, the way you manage and lead your team is what makes the biggest difference to how engaged the people in it are. It starts with you.

Are you leading a team or a group?

We tend to refer to the salespeople who work for a manager as a 'team,' but this can be misleading. A genuine team is a collection of people who are interdependent on one another for the achievement of a shared objective, such as a product development team would be. Salespeople aren't like that. They each have their own objectives and tend to work independently towards them. In fact, you might be more likely to think of your team as being made up of colleagues in marketing and other business functions, not the people who report into the same manager as you do.

That's not to say that fostering an element of team spirit isn't of benefit to your people, not least because it gives them a feeling of belonging and connectedness which (as we're soon to learn) is an important factor in how engaged they are. But it shouldn't be your main focus. I think of sales teams as sales groups. A group is a set of individuals who may carry out similar roles and work for the same manager, but they're independent of each other. I'll continue to refer to sales groups as sales teams because 'team' is the more accepted term, but it's helpful to see the difference.

If you want to create a high-growth culture and to achieve great performance from your salespeople, you have to see them as individuals who are unique in their own ways. This is central to how you interpret what we're about to explore in the field of motivation and engagement. For each one of your team, could you describe the following?

▶ Their career aspirations

▶ Their values

▶ Their talents, gifts, and skills

▶ Their communication style

▶ Their development needs

When I first start working with sales leaders, I often share this list with them and ask if they'd be able to fill out the answers for each member of their team. I suggest that you use it as well – it's a great way of measuring how well you really know your people. Without knowing the individuals in your team at this kind of level, how can you engage with them? How can you empower and mobilize them if you're not sure what's most important to them? Every person is motivated by different things, and it's your job to find out what they are.

What motivates salespeople (and what doesn't)

Engagement is closely linked to motivation – the reasons why people act in a certain way. If we're engaged, we feel motivated to do a good job, and if we're disengaged, we don't. Traditionally, the most common way that sales managers try to motivate their teams is through money. I've often heard the phrase, 'I want coin-operated salespeople,' which implies that the greater the financial incentive, the more they'll sell. I find this a frustrating assumption because Sales isn't just about money, nor are salespeople only motivated by it. In fact, as long as a salesperson is paid at their market rate, any extra amount isn't a motivation at all. That's because the money itself isn't important to them, it's *what the money does for them*.

The reliance on financial incentives in Sales can be a hard nut to crack, because many salespeople themselves are convinced that they're only motivated by money. I recently had a conversation with a highly experienced salesperson in which he told me that he happily made huge sacrifices in his personal life, such as missing his kids' sports matches and family barbecues, so that he could earn more money. I was shocked at this because, to me, nothing is worth missing those kinds of things. When I asked him if he really was okay with the situation, he replied that he often had to do it to provide for his family, so they had the essentials they needed. 'Ah,' I said. 'So, you're not doing it for the *money*, you're doing it to put food on the table for your kids.' Money was the enabler for him to play the important role of provider.

Maybe you're still thinking salespeople are motivated by money. If so, try asking yourself the following question. 'If I was offered a job I hated, but for a lot more money than I earn in Sales now, would I take it?' I doubt that you would. And here's another one: 'If I was paid twice as much as I am now, would I work twice as hard?' I think you probably wouldn't; after a while, the reward would feel normal, and you'd slip back into your habitual work style.

You could also try a little experiment: just pay your people more money and see what happens. If you gain better results, and they're sustainable, then great. But my guess is that at some point you'll hit a plateau and your return on investment will decline. Also, what happens when a competitor offers your top performer more money as an incentive to move? If money is all you've given them as a motivator, off they'll go.

Sales is a challenging environment to work in, but it can also be fun and rewarding. The concept of coin-operated salespeople assumes that not only is everyone motivated by money, but also that they're identical to one another. When managers take this approach, their teams become demotivated and disengaged, unwilling to put in extra effort when things aren't going well, or doing the minimum they can get away with. It can also lead them to leave their organization for somewhere that they perceive to be more sympathetic to their personal values and aims. It can be interesting to ask yourself what you think your individual team members would say that their motivation is based on. This is a test for how well you know them.

There are many studies that have been carried out on why people quit their jobs, but there's one which is evidence-based which I find to be highly informative.[7] It cites 11 reasons, of which the following are most relevant to Sales.

- **Lack of appreciation.** This is particularly important for younger workers, with nearly eight out of ten millennials saying that they'd look for new opportunities if they didn't feel appreciated. However, everyone wants to feel valued for their contribution, and a lack of this is the primary reason for people handing in their notice.

- **Feeling burnt out.** The main reasons for this are poor pay, unreasonable workloads, and overly long hours. It goes without saying that these factors are demotivating, but it's also worth thinking about how they're exacerbated by managers who firefight and don't plan ahead.

- **Poor mental health.** This can be caused by many factors but isn't helped by working in an environment in which people's personal values and motivations aren't taken into consideration. Long working hours, often caused by unrealistic demands and chaotic working environments, are also to blame.

- **Bad relationship with management.** A Gallup poll of over one million workers in the US found that having what they saw as a bad manager was the number one reason people quit.[8] You'll know from your own experience (good or bad) what an enormous difference it makes to have a manager who understands and appreciates you, as opposed to one who has a negative relationship with you. It can make the difference between you staying and leaving.

- **Lack of engagement.** We've already covered this!

- **Lack of career growth.** This is why your team's development is so important. When people aren't getting better at what they do, and aren't seeing opportunities to improve their circumstances, they can feel demotivated and leave.

You'll notice that a lack of money doesn't feature much at all in this list (neither does it in the full list of 11 reasons). What people want is reward (which is only partly financial), and recognition. Yes, they'll get their commission cheque when the deals close, but recognition goes beyond that. For instance, if you have a married team member who's done particularly well and you want to recognize their contribution, how about giving them a voucher for dinner for two to their favourite restaurant? Or, if one of your salespeople has worked all weekend to pull off a high-value sale, would a thank-you card to their partner for their sacrifice go down well? You're showing that you see them as whole people, not as coin-operated work machines. That means a lot, and it also brings rewards. Because how much more does the motivated employee produce for you, and how much does the demotivated one cost you?

Autonomy, competence, and relatedness

The motivating factors that we've looked at so far are mainly external ones, or what psychologists call 'extrinsic' motivators. Reward and recognition are things that come from outside us, whether it be from a manager, colleague, or loved one. Of course, we can always reward ourselves and give recognition to our own achievements, but that will only take us so far; we need the validation from others if they're to be true motivators.

Just as powerful, and in many ways more so, are 'intrinsic' motivators – the ones that come from within. Intrinsic motivation is not down to any anticipated reward, deadline, or outside pressure; in fact, it's continuous because it's built into our very identities. Researchers have spent a lot of time examining the factors that relate to intrinsic motivation because they know that they produce powerful results. They're the main drivers of the discretionary effort that I referred to earlier – the 'extra mile' that your people will go to if they feel engaged.

The three motivators I'm exploring here are the ones that psychologists Richard Ryan and Edward Deci have identified as being key to intrinsic motivation:[9]

1. Autonomy

2. Competence

3. Relatedness

Autonomy

This is the ability to have some level of control over our work, not only in terms of what we do but the way we do it. Giving autonomy to your team doesn't involve you abdicating your responsibility and allowing people to 'go rogue', but recognizes that being trusted to make their own decisions and decide their working style means a huge amount to them – maybe more than you realize. Autonomy within a framework can be powerful.

Because many salespeople are given a fair bit of freedom in how they carry out their work already, this is an area that you might assume is already catered for. However, try asking yourself the following questions to see if you offer as much autonomy to your people as you could.

- Do I expect my team to follow my way of doing things, or do I leave it up to them to decide how to complete their tasks?

- Do I allow people any freedom of choice over their working practices?

- Do I consult my team on how they would like to run our meetings?

Competence

We all like to feel good at what we do, and to know that we're getting better at it. As we've seen, one of the main reasons people leave a job is because they don't see enough development in themselves, whether it be in their skills or their career progress. This is why it's so important to focus on your team's training and development, whether it be through coaching or courses. Creating opportunities for people to improve makes them feel empowered and engaged.

Another part of feeling competent is knowing what your purpose is, and what you're being expected to achieve. This is something you can involve your team in creating. You could also explore what a high-growth team would look like if it was gaining the success it wanted. What would everyone in it be doing? How would they be acting? And imagine if you had a team with a jointly created vision of success that everyone felt equally passionate about achieving – how motivated would it be then?

Here are some questions to ask yourself to see if you're offering your people the chance to develop their competence.

- ▶ When I see someone doing something wrong, do I step in and correct them, or do I help them to see why it might not work?

- ▶ Do I regularly review people's performance levels to learn if they've improved their skills over time?

- ▶ Do I compare my salespeople only with each other, or do I look outside my organization to see how they'd compare with the best?

Relatedness

This is to do with feeling part of something bigger than ourselves, and having a connection with others that helps us to feel secure and supported. Relatedness can come not only from close colleagues but also from the organization as a whole.

It's important that your people have good relationships with each other, and especially with you. This involves you making time for, and listening to, one another. It's also essential that salespeople understand how their work contributes to the team as a whole, and also to the business; this creates a connection between their individual achievements and the bigger picture that they're a part of.

When Clive Woodward took over as England Rugby Coach in 1997, he asked his players to determine their own playbook for how they'd operate as a team. They came up with rules, such as turning up five minutes early for every team meeting, or not having mobile phones in the room. These became the standard that they worked to, and the 'policing' of the rules was carried out by the team itself. A manager gets out of their team what they tolerate. If you tolerate poor performance, that's what you'll have. So having some standards to work to – some things that you will and won't accept – is helpful.

Key to relatedness is the concept of psychological safety. This is a belief that we won't be criticized for speaking up about ideas, questions, or concerns, and that it's okay to make honest mistakes. It enables us to take risks and try new things without the fear of being punished or humiliated if we fail. Feeling psychologically safe gives your people the confidence to know that they can be themselves, which is important for their sense of autonomy too. It also allows them to admit when they don't know something, which is central to their journey of self-development. And it's essential if you want to create a high-growth team culture, because a belief that failure is only the first step to improvement is integral to having a growth mindset.

Here are some questions to ask yourself to judge how much you're encouraging a feeling of relatedness in your people.

> ▷ How often do I set aside time to speak with, and listen to, my team members on a one-to-one basis, with the focus simply on them?

> ▷ Do I connect their individual objectives to those of the organization as a whole?

> ▷ Is there a mutual feeling of trust between me and my team?

Overall, people want the opportunity to do things their own way as much as possible, to grow and become better at what they do, and to belong to something bigger than themselves. Are you creating the environment that enables that to happen? Leaders who inspire confidence do this as a natural part of their role. They give people the autonomy to make decisions with clear goals and accountability, they continually foster people's development, and they're visibly committed to the organization and to their own teams.

In the next chapter you'll learn one of the most powerful tools around for developing and getting the best out of your people: coaching.

Key takeaways

> ▷ Engagement is a critical factor for driving long-term success, improving loyalty, productivity, and performance.

> ▷ Sales teams are made up of unique individuals, and effective leadership begins with understanding each person's motivations, values, and goals.

- Financial incentives are less impactful than fostering intrinsic motivators like autonomy, competence, and relatedness.

- Creating psychological safety and a culture of trust enables teams to innovate, grow, and perform at their best.

- Engaged leaders inspire confidence and commitment by balancing individual development with organizational objectives.

Chapter 7
The power of coaching

I've mentioned the value of coaching a number of times so far, and here's where I explain what it is, why it works, and how to do it. I've been a qualified coach for well over a decade and have coached hundreds of sales leaders in that time, and I'm looking forward to sharing my knowledge and experience with you.

What is coaching? The definition I most like is from Sir John Whitmore, co-founder of the GROW model of coaching that's so popular today. He said: 'Coaching is unlocking a person's potential to maximize their own performance. It is helping them to learn, rather than teaching them.'[1] To him, central to it is the act of seeing people in terms of their future potential, not their past performance. I agree wholeheartedly with that, because I've witnessed first-hand the transformational effects of coaching.

Why coach people?

Given that autonomy, competence, and relatedness are critical motivators, it follows that any way of developing your people should build on them rather than work against them. Coaching achieves this on all fronts.

First, it's a way of empowering people – giving them the opportunity to think for themselves and decide which action will move them forward.

This encourages a sense of autonomy, improves their competence, and bolsters their sense of relatedness through the trust that it creates between manager and salesperson. If a person sees that their manager believes in their potential and is dedicated to supporting them, it builds a bond that being sent on a training course can never achieve.

In addition, there's a significant amount of research proving that coaching has a positive effect on performance, particularly within a sales environment. Research from the Corporate Executive Board (CEB) shows that a salesperson can achieve an average of 19% higher sales when they have an effective sales coach. Sales organizations that embrace coaching can improve win rates by 28% and quota attainment by 10%.[2] And people who receive as little as three hours coaching a month significantly outperform people who receive none.

Although coaching is sometimes referred to as a soft skill – all warm and fluffy – it's actually a hard skill in that it has a direct impact on performance. It's not about having a nice chat, it's an enabler for people to realize their potential so that they can improve how they do their jobs in the long term.

Despite the overwhelming benefits of coaching, I don't see much evidence that organizations are buying into it within their sales departments. Why is that? In my experience, one of the key reasons is sales managers' resistance to it. When I've explored this with people, I've found that it comes down to three factors.

1. They don't understand the full benefits of coaching. Despite the compelling research data, it can't replace the experience of practising it for real and witnessing the results.

2. Most sales managers don't understand what coaching is and aren't sure how to do it. They might assume that it's a way of carrying out reviews or checking people are okay, or even a subtle form of manipulation.

3. They think that they don't have the time to coach. This is partly because they don't see the value in it and struggle to appreciate what it is, so they don't prioritize it. And it's partly because they don't see that their role is not to be a problem-solver for

their people, but to invest time in coaching to create a more productive, empowered, and motivated sales team. This will eventually free up their time, because the results from coaching are so much more sustainable than quick fixes.

It's worth exploring the 'lack of time' objection further, because it's so prevalent. Of course, if you tell someone what to do, you may well achieve an instant result. But how will that person take what they've learned and apply it to other situations in the future? Coaching helps them to develop a new skill, or to have a better awareness of what's been holding them back, and this makes the learning repeatable. That's why coaching should be one of your big rocks. You shouldn't be trying to fit it in around everything else but be making it an integral part of leading your people so that other tasks have to work around it.

You can also integrate coaching into many of your regular activities. This is something that I'll explain in more depth in later chapters, but so you can see what I mean, take forecasting as an example. If you're like most sales managers I come across, you do this by asking your salespeople to give you their personal forecasts which you then discuss with them. But is there another way? Could you make the process of forecasting a coaching conversation, so that it adds value to your people? You could look not just at the numbers but at how the person is going to achieve them. What challenges might they encounter? How could they overcome them? Through this you're transforming an administrative task into a learning opportunity, in a way that both develops the person and delivers the figures you need.

How to coach

Because coaching is a process it can be helpful to have a framework to base it on, especially when you first start. The system I use the most is GROW, which was developed in the 1980s by Sir John Whitmore and his colleagues at Performance Consultants International. He wrote the book *Coaching for Performance*, which you can read if you'd like to gain a more in-depth understanding of the process.

The GROW model

GROW is an acronym for four components:

- ▶ **G**oal
- ▶ **R**eality
- ▶ **O**ptions
- ▶ **W**ay forward

GROW gives you a structure for a coaching conversation. It helps you to enable someone to learn about why they're finding a situation and problem difficult, and what they can do to overcome it. You're encouraging them to take responsibility for improving themselves by supporting them with the tool, and also holding them accountable for taking the necessary actions as a next step.

One of the core beliefs in coaching is that the person you're supporting already has the answers to their problem. They almost certainly know what they should be doing to succeed, but they're not doing it. Something is getting in the way. Tim Gallwey, who's worked closely with Whitmore, uses an equation to describe this:

$$Performance = Capacity - Interference$$

Interference is often the mindset of the person – the thinking that's holding them back without them being aware of it – such as self-limiting beliefs and imposter syndrome. This is the 'noise' that's getting in the way of them achieving their potential. Coaching enables them to quieten the noise so as to improve their performance and make use of their full capacity.

Let's look at the four elements of GROW in turn.

Goal

This is where you focus on what the person you're coaching wants to achieve. It can work on two levels; there's the long-term goal (for instance, they want to improve their sales closing skills) and the short-term goal (what they want to get out of that particular session). It's important that whatever outcome you agree on is SMART (Specific,

Measurable, Actionable, Relevant, and Timebound), and also that it matters to the person – it should inspire them in some way.

Here are some examples of questions that you could ask to establish the goal.

- What would you like to focus on right now?
- Where do you want to get to?
- When you look back on this session, what would you like to have achieved?
- How will you know you've achieved it?

Reality

Next, ask the person to describe their current reality. Although this might sound as if it's for your benefit rather than theirs, the opposite is true. In fact, you're not wanting to understand too much about what's going on for them because it can lead you to get sucked into their problem. The purpose of them describing the situation is for them to put it into words, which is something that they've probably not done until this moment. This helps them to identify some of the obstacles that they're facing, some of which might be hidden.

Here are some examples of questions that you could ask to help them explore their current reality.

- What have you tried so far?
- What's got you to this position?
- What's worked and what hasn't?
- What else is hindering you?

Options

This is the stage at which you help them to move from where they are now, to the place they're trying to reach. As the name implies, you're looking at as many potential solutions as possible, without any censorship or conditions attached. You're not worrying about whether something is feasible or whether the person wants to do it, you're simply asking: 'What could it be?' The idea is to get them thinking, because when you encourage them to think it will help them to apply what they learn to new situations in the future, not just this one. Coaching should always have an impact on more than one scenario.

Given that, like your team member, you're also an expert in sales, you might find yourself tempted to offer suggestions at this stage. That's fine if you have something useful to add, but only if you treat your ideas as being of no higher value than theirs, and only if you give them after they've already done the talking.

Here are some examples of questions that you could ask to help them come up with multiple options.

> What could be your first step?

> What would you suggest to a colleague who was having the same problem as you?

> If you couldn't fail, what would you do?

> If time and money were no barrier, what action could you take?

Way forward

This is sometimes also referred to as 'Will', as in, 'What *will* you do?' It's when you narrow down the options to the one (or ones) that the person will definitely put into action. As part of this process, you discuss which actions are most feasible and whether they'll help them to achieve their goal. Then you encourage them to take ownership of how they'll move forward.

Here are some examples of questions that you could ask to help them to commit to a set of actions.

> What will you do first, second, and third?

> What might stop you from doing this?

> How motivated do you feel to take this action?

> What help do you need to achieve it?

This is a high-level overview of GROW, and I hope you find it useful. You'll only really learn how to use it when you put it into practice, though, so let's go through an example situation which should help you to see how it works. Please bear in mind that this is a simplified version of what might in reality be a longer and more nuanced coaching conversation.

An example conversation

It's Tuesday morning and one of your sales team approaches your desk. 'I have a problem. Can you help?'

'Certainly,' you say. 'I have about 20 minutes to spare. Let's spend that time talking about it. What would you like to get out of this conversation?'

'I've got this great opportunity with a new customer, but they're not returning my calls. I feel stuck. I guess that what I'd like to get out of this conversation is at least two ways of dealing with it over the next week so that I can move the situation forward.' (They've set their goal).

'Okay, so tell me what you've done up to now. What do you see as being the issue?'

'Well, I've sent a quote, after which I've emailed twice and left a voice message for the customer to call me back. None have been responded to, and I don't know why. There's also a complication in that I'm pretty sure they have a new purchasing manager who's getting involved in the background, and I've not been able to speak to them.' (They've given their reality).

'Do you have any other thoughts around this? Any insights?'

'I guess I feel a bit intimidated by the person I've been dealing with. She's very senior in the organization and I'm worried she's going to see me as a pest. I suppose I could just take a deep breath and give her one last try.'

'I see. If you were giving advice to someone else on your team who had this problem, what would you say?'

The salesperson smiles. 'I'd say, "Remember the value you have to offer this customer – you're helping them to solve a big problem. Focus on that rather than on your own insecurities."'

'And does that help?'

'Yes, it does. I've just thought, I could also see if our own purchasing director Doug knows anything about this new guy – he's in an online networking group of purchasers and they might know each other. If I had a name, I could approach him direct to see if I can address any issues he may have.'

'That sounds like a good option. I have another idea; would you like to hear it?'

'Of course!'

'You could create a slimmed-down version of the spec sheet you've already sent the customer, which makes the key features easier to understand. Then give her a call to ask if she'd prefer to use this when she talks to purchasing. Not only might it be exactly what she's wanting without realizing it, but it also gives you a reasonable excuse to call her again without it being another chaser call.'

'That sounds like a great option, thanks.' (Now all options are on the table.)

'So, my next question is, what are you going to do, and when by?'

'I like the idea of the new spec sheet, so I'll create that by Friday and give the customer a call then. I'll also speak to Doug this afternoon, as I have a meeting over his way.'

'Do you need any support to make this happen?'

'I don't think so. Although it might be helpful to ask Sarah in Marketing to look over my spec sheet as she always has a good way of presenting things. I'll see if she can give some input.'

'Brilliant. Let's touch base on how it's gone on Friday afternoon after you've called the customer again. I'm on the road that day, so I'll expect a call on my mobile.' (The salesperson is now committed to specific and timebound actions, with accountability added in.)

As a final note, you should always check that the person did what they committed to and ask them how it went. There are likely to be three types of outcome, and each of them can lead to a new coaching conversation.

1. They took the action that they said they'd take and achieved the outcome they wanted. Celebrate this, and also ask them what they learned so they can use this knowledge in other situations.

2. They took the action but didn't get the results they were after. You can still celebrate the fact that they did it, but examine the reasons why it didn't work so they can take something useful from the situation.

3. They didn't take the action. If that happens, don't criticize or judge them. Instead, ask them what got in the way. Did something happen that removed the need for the action? Did they not feel capable of doing it? Explore the issues and ask them what they've learned from them.

Part of the power of coaching is that it helps people not just to solve the problem they have right now, but to apply what they've learned to other situations in the future. This is why it's important to close the loop by asking them what they've got out of the actions they've taken. Otherwise, in a month's time, they'll come to you with exactly the same issue but in a different guise.

Telling a person what to do versus coaching

The easy option for the sales manager would have been to say to their team member, 'Just try this', or 'You could do that'. But the problem here is that, in most cases, the salesperson knows what they should be doing, they're just not doing it. So, if you tell them what to do it's unlikely that they'll carry it out, because there's something else getting in the way. This is what the coaching conversation is designed to uncover.

The other danger of telling a person what to do is that you create a learned dependency, whereby every time they have a problem they come to you for advice. They stop thinking for themselves and transfer the responsibility for their actions onto you. This causes three issues. The first is that you become a bottleneck; if you're not around to ask for help, they take no action. The second is that they assume you have all the answers, which you don't. What worked for you in the past might not work for them in this specific situation today. And the third is that because you've encouraged them to put the responsibility for making decisions onto you, if they follow your advice and it doesn't work, it's your fault. Alternatively, if it does work it's to your credit, not theirs. You want them to feel empowered, not to blame (or praise) someone else. If you always make their decisions for them, you'll end up becoming a firefighter and a fixer, which is the opposite of what an inspiring leader should be.

A final reason for encouraging people to come up with their own ideas is that we always feel more enthusiastic about actioning our own initiatives than the ones that have been suggested to us. I remember a conversation with a sales manager called Dennis from the Netherlands. When he heard me make this point he smiled and said, 'I'll give you an example. I was in my home office the other day and saw that my desk was a bit messy, so I made a promise to myself that when I finished for the day I'd tidy it up and give everything a wipe down. It would make the whole place look better. Then my wife came in with a cup of coffee. As she put it down she said, "Dennis, I think you should tidy up your desk. It's looking a bit of a mess." And I felt an instant resistance to doing it. No way was I going to tidy up my desk now! It's ridiculous because I adore my wife and respect her, and she was right about my desk. But just because she suggested it, I didn't do it.'

Putting coaching into practice

It's important to realize that, just as you can't learn to swim by reading a book, so you have to practise coaching if you want to become good. At first it might feel a bit strange and artificial, and you'll make mistakes, but the more you do it the better you'll get and the more it will be integrated into the way you work. In time you might want to work with a coaching trainer who will help you develop your coaching skills to a higher level.

Another thing about coaching is that it can feel as if you're doing it as an activity. But coaching is something you're 'being,' not 'doing.' It's a mindset shift. As a coach, you show unconditional positive regard to your people; you believe that they can be better than they are, and you help them to achieve that. Enabling people to think for themselves is part of leadership, and as a leader, your aim is for your people to lead themselves through their own learning. That's a key part of creating a high-growth culture.

Coaching is the best way I know to stop being a sticking-plaster manager, and to become someone who leads their salespeople to develop themselves through continuous learning and improvement. It's more than worth your while to give it a go.

Key takeaways

- Coaching empowers team members to think independently, fostering skills they can apply across diverse situations.

- While coaching may require more time initially, it creates sustainable outcomes that reduce future managerial interventions.

- Coaching enhances engagement by developing autonomy, competence, and trust, which are key drivers of motivation.

- The GROW model provides a practical framework for effective coaching, helping leaders guide team members toward solutions and growth.

- True coaching is a mindset that leaders cultivate, combining practice with continuous learning to inspire a high-growth culture.

PART 3

THE THREE ROLES
OF THE SALES LEADER

You've spent time reflecting on yourself as a leader and understanding how to build a high-performing team. Now it's time to bring all of that learning to life – to shift from understanding to execution. This part of the book is about applying what you know across the full spectrum of your role as a sales leader.

If you cast your mind back to Chapter 5, you'll remember that I introduced the three core roles that define the work of a sales leader. Almost everything you do will fall into one of these three areas:

1. The customer leader
2. The business leader
3. The people leader

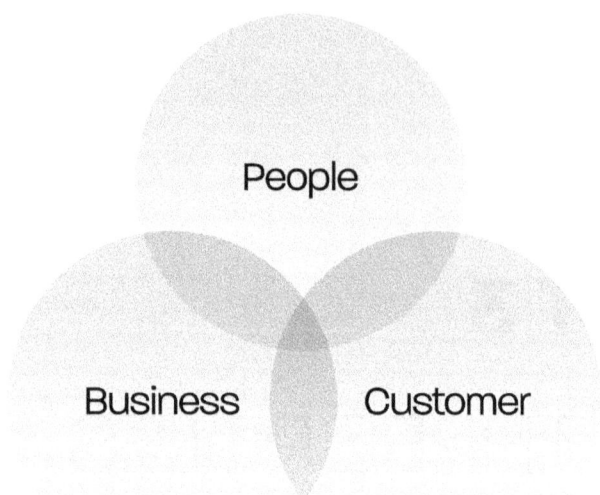

These roles aren't just functional categories – they represent the three key dimensions of modern sales leadership. The people role is where you recruit, coach, and develop your team. The business role is where you manage forecasts, reporting, and internal execution. And the customer role is where you build strategic relationships and help your people win.

I'm making some assumptions here, but I suspect the role you enjoy most is the customer role – because it's closest to what you did as a salesperson. The business leader role might be the one you like least, as it tends to involve administrative tasks and internal pressure. And the people leader role? That's often the one managers feel most unsure about – it matters, but it's easy to push aside when time is tight or skills are lacking.

That's why I'm addressing the roles in the opposite order to how I introduced them. We'll start with the people leader, then explore the business leader, and finally dive into the customer leader. Each chapter will offer practical guidance on what leadership looks like in that domain – and how you can step into it with more clarity and confidence.

But I want you to do more than just treat these roles as separate silos. The magic happens in the *overlap* – where people, business, and customer leadership come together. Most sales leaders separate these areas without meaning to: they 'do' people stuff one day, and 'business stuff' the next. That kind of thinking leads to fragmentation and burnout.

My goal is to help you see the power of integration. When you blend the roles together, each one strengthens the others. You'll lead with more impact, your team will perform with more consistency, and your time will be better spent. That's the hallmark of a true sales leader.

Let's dive in.

Chapter 8
The people leader

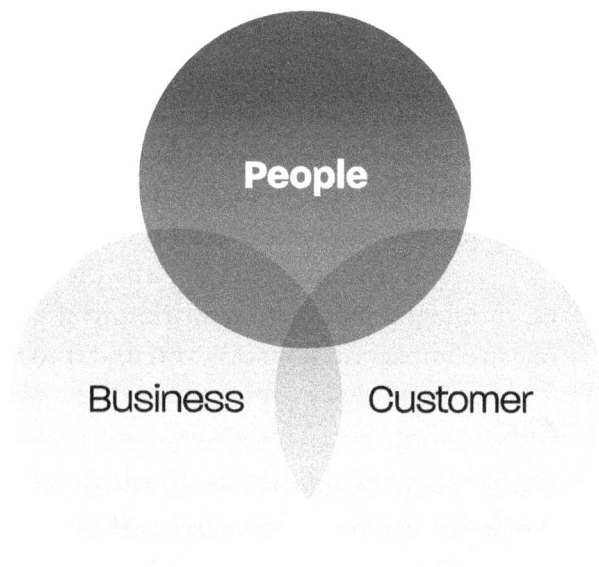

People

Business   Customer

People – can't live with them, can't live without them. Sometimes it feels that way, doesn't it? You spend your time trying to get your team to do what you need them to do, with only partial success, then one of your best salespeople leaves and you have to start all over again with someone new. As author Gerald Weinberg once put it, 'no matter what the problem is, it's always a people problem.' This is why the people leader role can seem like a burden. And yet, as we've explored in various ways so far, it's actually the key to unlocking your sales success.

When thinking about the people leader, it's helpful to break the role down into three main areas of activity:

1. Recruitment and onboarding

2. Developing your people

3. Career and succession planning

As we cover these areas, you'll learn how to prevent 'people problems' arising in the first place. And it goes further than that. When you know how to bring in the right team members, how to plan their development, and how to ensure that they continue to evolve in their careers, you'll be able to say that your people are your greatest strength. You'll wonder how you ever cope without them.

Recruitment and onboarding

If you've ever inherited a team of unmotivated, poorly trained, or difficult to manage salespeople, you'll understand that attracting and recruiting top quality employees is a critical part of the people leader's role. Conversely, if you have a high-quality team in place, half of your job is done for you. It makes that much of a difference. And yet so many sales managers see recruitment as a necessary evil – something they have to squeeze into their already hectic week. In fact, it should be an integral part of your work, and if you get it right it will have a massive impact on how easy you find it to reach your sales objectives.

ABR

You may have heard the saying 'ABC' – Always Be Closing. As you can probably imagine, I don't agree with this outdated idea, but what I am keen on is an alternative: 'ABR.' This stands for Always Be Recruiting.

What does ABR really mean? Most managers only start thinking about recruitment when they have a vacancy or need to expand their team. My view, however, is that recruitment works best when it's woven into your everyday activities as a habit or routine. It's not something that you start and stop, it's something that you're always doing.

The idea behind ABR is that you always have some activity going on that's to do with bringing new people into your team. I call this building 'bench strength.' Then, when the time comes to recruit, you already have a number of people who you know are a good fit. The advantages of this are twofold: you're able to fill vacancies more quickly, and you're less tempted to retain poor performers because of worries about opening a temporary gap in your team.

Many people find this a difficult concept because they're not sure where to start. They think that they don't know anyone suitable or don't have enough contacts, but it's likely that your network is wider than you assume. How about:

- LinkedIn connections
- Friends and family connections

- ▷ People you meet at work-related events

- ▷ High performers you come across in sales magazines, online articles, or podcasts

I'm sure you can think of more. The point is to keep your eyes and ears open, because then you'll find yourself bumping into potential recruits all the time. Nor should you restrict yourself to your own sector or industry; sometimes the best ideas come from elsewhere. And be careful to include those who are different from you and your existing team in various ways – you're not wanting to create a bank of clones.

When you spot someone you'd like to speak with, it's best to arrange a conversation in which you're completely honest with them. Tell them that although you don't have a vacancy at the moment, you're always on the lookout for top talent and that you've approached them because you think they might be a great addition to your team. Find out more about them and ask if they're interested in your business. Are they willing to be part of your 'bench'? If so, keep in touch, and when the time comes, they'll be one more person you can contact as a potential recruit.

But I can't do that because...

The main challenge with this idea is that many organizations, particularly large corporates, don't allow you to start the recruitment process until there's a vacancy or a sign-off for a new role. With HR rules, advertising, approvals, and interviews, there's always a gap between someone resigning and you being able to bring in a replacement. And yet your sales target doesn't go away; you still carry the quota for the person who's not there while you're doing all this.

It can seem an impossible position to be in, but it isn't. For a start, you might be able to challenge the established procedures at your organization. You're a leader – that's what leaders do. And second, being constrained is as much of an internal as an external concept. You don't have to wait until your recruitment requisition form is signed before you start reaching out to people and building your network. You can do it now.

My questions to you are: how often are you having ABR conversations? Do you know who's in the market for a new role? Do you think they might be right for you, and vice versa? Have you approached them? If one of your team was to resign tomorrow, who would fill the gap? Could you name them? And do you know how long would it take to put them in place? If your answers are in the negative, you're going to face a difficult situation when you next need to recruit someone. So why not reach out to some new people today?

By the way, does the concept and approach of ABR sound familiar? Of course it does, it's what you did with prospects and customers when you were a salesperson. The same skills and concepts apply when attracting top talent as they do when attracting new customers. It's about pipeline building, only a different type of pipeline.

Create a robust hiring process

I saw a post on LinkedIn that made me laugh: 'Hiring for salespeople is so hard. They interview like Tom Cruise, and after three months on the payroll they turn into Mr Bean.'

It's true – *of course* salespeople interview well, it's what they're trained to do. And it's the very reason you need a robust and repeatable recruitment process that you can improve on over time. Very few sales managers have been formally trained in interviewing. Most have their own way of recruiting, but it's usually one that feels natural to them – it's not necessarily the most effective. If you create a process that works and is consistent, you'll hire better people and also be able to spot when it needs updating.

So, what does the ideal process look like? That will depend on your particular circumstances, but it should follow this broad and simple outline:

1. Decide what good looks like

2. Screen and recruit candidates against your ideal profile

3. Onboard your new recruit

1. Decide what good looks like

You probably have a feel for what your ideal salesperson would be like in terms of their experience, personality, and the way they do things. But have you ever been specific about this? And have you tested your assumptions in a scientific way?

I've long admired the views of recruitment and careers expert Roger Philby, founder of The Chemistry Group, a business specializing in the best ways of recruiting people.[1] He's profiled high, medium, and low performers in every part of the world across multiple sectors and roles, and through the data he's amassed, has come to the conclusion that the least reliable predictor of future performance is a candidate's previous experience. That's right: the worst thing you can do is to recruit someone just because of what they've done elsewhere.

The model that The Chemistry Group has come up with instead is to think about the people who thrive in your organization. What makes them different to the people who don't? Then write down each factor on an individual sticky note. It could be that they're 'hardworking' or have 'attention to detail,' for instance – try to be specific. Then, when the notes are done, you can think about which of the following categories you would put them in:

- **Intellect** – measures the speed at which you take in, retain, and process information.

- **Personality** – looks at the 'Big 5' personality traits that underpin your values in the workplace.

- **Motivations** – focuses on identifying the kinds of activities you will be motivated to do and your preference for how you go about doing that task.

- **Behaviours** – assesses your 'working habits.' What you 'will do' as opposed to what you 'can do.'

- **Experience** – what you have done before, or what you are 'capable of doing.'

For example, if one of your sticky notes says 'confident' it would go into the Personality category, and if it says 'results focused' it would go in the Motivations category. Now imagine you're carrying out this exercise for a new recruit. I'd be pretty sure that few of your sticky notes would fall into the Experience area; they'd almost all be allocated to Personality, Motivations, and Behaviours. And yet most sales leaders recruit according to Experience, which is why hiring can be so hit and miss.

This isn't to say that experience isn't relevant – it has some bearing on who you recruit. But it's not the number of years that a person has under their belt that you should focus on, nor only what they've done or know. It's why they did what they did, and what they learned from it that can be transferred to your organization. In other words, the journey to the results they gained, rather than only the results themselves.

It's also worth considering what kind of attitude you want your new hire to have, because two key traits that are critical to salespeople's success are positivity and optimism. In his book *Positive Intelligence*, coach Shirzad Chamine uses his research to reveal that salespeople who have what he calls a high PQ (Positive Intelligence Quotient) achieve 37% more sales.[2]

Chamine's findings are borne out by Dr Martin Seligman of the University of Pennsylvania, who's investigated the impact of optimism on success.[3] He tells the story of how he added an optimism test into a company's recruitment process for salespeople, with astonishing results. In the first year, those who passed both his optimism test and the company's own sales aptitude test outperformed those who only passed the aptitude test (we'll call them 'competent pessimists') by 8%. In their second year it was 31%. As a result of this, Seligman was able to persuade the business to hire 'super-optimists' – candidates who scored extremely highly on the optimism test but failed the aptitude test. These salespeople outperformed the competent pessimists by 21% in the first year and an incredible 57% in year two. Optimism was shown to correlate heavily with a salesperson's success, even if they didn't have that much in the way of selling skills when they started the job.

This makes sense to me. I see positivity and optimism as the ability to get the best out of every situation, rather than being derailed by uncontrollable events. When you have salespeople who look at things in a positive light, not only are they naturally inclined to turn difficult situations around, they're also likely to have a growth mindset which encourages them to improve. With a team of such people, just think what you could achieve.

Deciding what good looks like, in a scientific rather than instinctive way, is crucial for creating an objective profile for your ideal candidate. However, there's no one profile that works for all organizations. McKinsey, for instance, did some research with over 15,000 salespeople across 100 companies.[4] The results revealed that organizations with the fastest growth knew who their top performers were, and what personality traits and skills corresponded with success. One insurance company's most successful salespeople were 'ambitious solution sellers,' who were assertive and good at converting objections to opportunities. At a telecoms company, on the other hand, the highest performers were 'expert insiders,' who were great at explaining the product to customers. This exercise of working out who the top performers were and analyzing the factors behind it can prove eye-opening, as one media company discovered. After it profiled its sales roles, it learned that 40% of its new hires had a low performer profile, and only 10% had the characteristics aligning with top performers.

This shows how important it is to objectively analyze the qualities of the people you want to hire. So many people recruit on gut feel or by looking at someone's previous experience, but that isn't the way to ensure that you bring in those who will perform the best for you.

2. Screen and recruit candidates against your ideal profile

A client recently told me that one of the salespeople they'd hired had gone through nine interviews. I was amazed. 'Why nine?' I asked. I'm all for hiring slowly enough to be thorough, but this seemed excessive. Every process should have multiple stages to it, but you need to be clear what the purpose of each stage is. In this case the company hadn't clarified what they wanted to achieve at each stage, which is why they had to back-track to cover off areas that had been missed. It also suggested to me that they weren't sure what kind of person they were looking for in the first place; if they had been, it would have been easy to see earlier on whether the candidate was right.

Psychometric testing can play a useful part in recruitment. I suggest that you ask people to take a test before you interview them, rather than the other way around, as it's more cost-effective that way. Interviews are, in most cases, the most expensive part of recruiting because they take up time, so testing beforehand can weed out unsuitable candidates before you see them. It also allows you to use the test to inform your interview, exploring any issues it's thrown up. You don't have to use the test as a binary 'pass or fail'. If there is deviation from your ideal profile, consider if this is something that is trainable like a skill or piece of knowledge versus a deep character trait.

Finally, when you make your decision, it needs to be a 'hell yeah' for you to offer someone a job. If it's a 'maybe', it's a 'no'. When you're clear on what good looks like and you've developed (and evolved) a robust recruitment process, you should feel confident that they're the right person. The majority of people problems come from bringing in a salesperson who isn't quite right and persuading yourself that they'll probably be okay once they've had some training. Have you ever done that? If it worked out well, I'm pleased for you (although it was probably a stroke of luck). And if it didn't go so well, you know the reason why. Often the pressure to recruit someone who will do for now comes from having to fill a gap, but once you're ABRing you'll have a bank of great candidates to choose from.

Is all this really necessary?

You may be muttering to yourself, 'Surely this is overkill? Selling is practically the only job in the world where someone's performance is transparently obvious – all you have to do is look at their figures. Why wouldn't I just bring in a top salesperson from another organization and have done with it?'

My answer is that if this is the approach you've taken and every hire you've made has been successful, then great – don't change it. But if you repeatedly find yourself bringing in people who seem like Tom Cruise but turn out to be Mr Bean, there's a problem. And it lies not with them, but with you. Just because someone tops the sales charts somewhere else, doesn't mean that they'll do the same in your organization. They might have happened to be in the right place at the right time, with the right customers (in other words, they were lucky). They may have worked with a different sales system, which played to their strengths. Or their personality and attitude was right for their previous place but might not translate well to yours. There are all sorts of reasons why high performers in one organization aren't necessarily best for another; you need to decide what personality, motivations, and behaviours are right for you, then make sure that anyone you hire has them in abundance.

3. Onboard your new recruit

When you receive an acceptance from your 'hell yeah' candidate, it's a fist pump moment. 'Thank heaven I have someone arriving in a couple of months,' you think, 'I can relax now.' However, I see onboarding a new hire as an integral part of the recruitment process, because until that person is installed and up and running, it isn't complete.

The quality of your onboarding plays a major role in how quickly recruits get up to speed. Research from CSO Insights suggests that it can take seven to nine months for a salesperson to reach the achievement level you're looking for, but with a robust process that can be reduced to three months.[5] There's also evidence that high quality onboarding makes it likely that your recruit will stay for longer, because it sets the tone for what their experience of working in the organization will be. And from your point of view, the onboarding period also allows you to identify at an early stage whether the person you've brought in is the right choice – both for you and them. If you don't have a system for deciding this you may not find out until later, when it becomes much more painful to say goodbye.

A robust onboarding process

In most companies, onboarding is rarely a positive, engaging experience. Often it's a collection of ad hoc activities, such as 'here's your laptop' and 'go and see these people in departments x, y, and z as soon as you can.' Even when it's well organized, it's not exactly fun. Worse still is when sales managers abdicate responsibility for the process to HR or Sales Enablement; this is unlikely to work well for you and is also unsatisfactory for the recruit because you'll be semi-strangers to each other when it's over.

As with hiring, you need a clearly defined onboarding process, from the moment the candidate accepts your offer to the time when they're fully up and running. Here are some things to think about when you create your own.

- What does the process look like overall?

- What should happen in week one, week two, and so on?

- What do you expect them to know, and have done, by the end of each week?

- How will you measure whether they've achieved it and what happens if they haven't?

- Are there ways of reducing the time it takes for the recruit to bed in?

- How can you make the period fun and interesting?

The key is to be able to measure and test your process at the end of each week and month, because what's measured can be improved. If your recruit hasn't completed all the activities you've set, or doesn't seem to know everything they should, what's the reason? Is the problem with your process, or with them? If you're measuring it, at least you'll know that there's an issue to deal with.

It's also important to make your expectations clear. A company I talked to in the US went on a mass recruitment drive for salespeople, and managed to hire almost all the ones they wanted. They were delighted, but after a few weeks they sensed that some of them weren't performing well. It turned out that no-one had made clear to the new hires what was expected of them, so naturally they performed at different levels and in varying ways. This problem actually went further back than that, in that no-one had defined what a good salesperson looked like at the recruitment stage.

Ideas for easy and effective onboarding

From my experience of onboarding people, there are many ways that you can make it a useful and enjoyable time for your new hires. Here's a small collection of ideas to help you.

Add variety. It's good to include a mix of learning methods; this ensures that you capture every learning style and keeps things fun. As well as face-to-face meetings you can have online courses, buddying with colleagues from various departments, and quizzes to test your hire's knowledge.

Start early. Rather than beginning the process on week one, is there a week minus one? Are there some activities you could ask them to do before they join, such as research, online learning, or digesting presentations that you send them? This can be applied both to internal hires and external ones who are working their notice.

Make it real. Incorporate some of the activities that you'd normally do with your recruit when they're up and running, such as your forecasting one-to-ones. It helps to set expectations for when they're fully part of the team.

Do it as a group. When someone new starts, you're likely to ask them to meet with key people in different parts of your business. That's a good thing but think about it from the perspective of the people they're seeing. If yours is a large organization those people will probably play host to a stream of recruits every week, which is a drain on their time. It's no wonder that they're often 'too busy' to meet your new hire. There's a way around this, which is to have each new hire start on the same day of the month. You can then arrange their introductory meetings as a group, which is time-efficient for everyone. So, the Head of Marketing knows that on the third Tuesday of every month they'll meet with new people from Sales (and maybe other departments as well); if it happens that there are none that month, they'll get their two hours back. This also gives more seasoned salespeople the opportunity to refresh their knowledge by joining in if they want to.

Developing your people

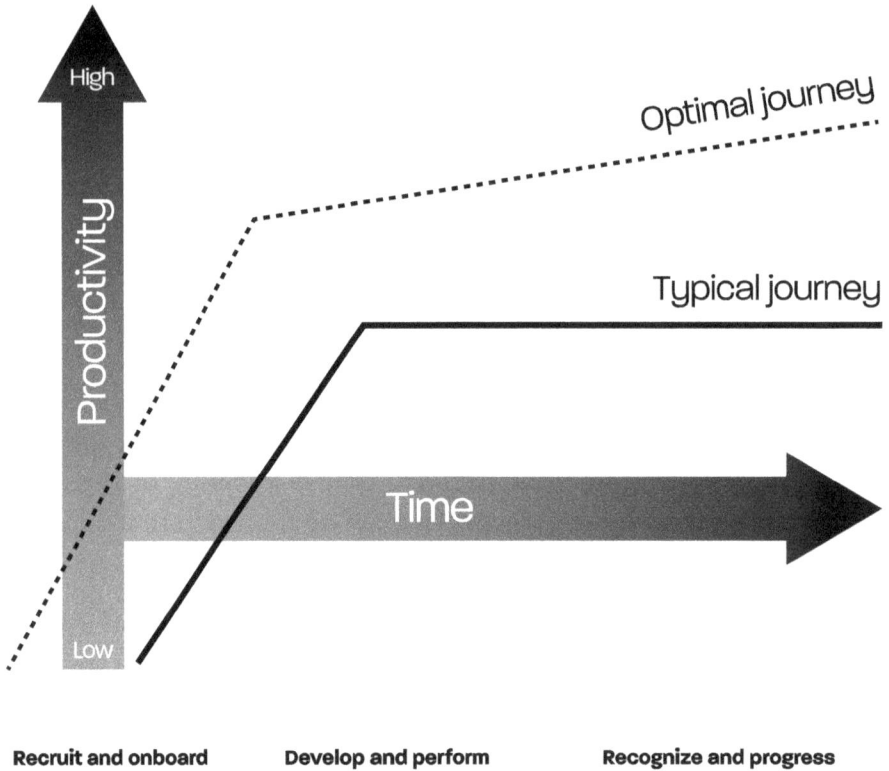

Recruit and onboard   Develop and perform   Recognize and progress

Let's think of developing your people as a journey. It starts with choosing the right employees to bring in, continues as they're onboarded, and carries on until they leave your team, at which point they're hopefully ready to move onto to the next stage of their career. It's your responsibility to keep that journey of growth alive, by creating constant opportunities for them to learn. Through this, you're helping to foster the three motivational factors that we talked about in Chapter 6: autonomy, competence, and relatedness. Autonomy because when they take charge of their own learning, they feel independent and in control; competence because continuous learning improves their skills; and relatedness because when learning is treated as a team activity it brings people together. Here are some areas to think about.

Personal development plans

Doing a job doesn't automatically make you better at it. I passed my driving test back in 1988 – a frighteningly long time ago when I think about it. Since then, I've driven an enormous number of miles (as a salesperson I was doing around 40,000 a year), but if I'm honest, I'm not much better a driver today than I was about a year after I jettisoned my L plates. This is known as a Performance Plateau, the point where our progress and improvement levels off. There are only two ways to learn through doing: when something goes wrong, or if you purposely analyze your actions. Learning through things going wrong can be helpful, but you obviously don't want to rely on that. The alternative is to decide to learn in a conscious way, and this is what a personal development plan can help with.

There's a quote from coaching expert Jim Rohn that I love: 'In one year's time, you will arrive. The question is, where?' This goes to the heart of why personal development plans are important: they take the luck out of whether or not learning takes place. Every member of your team, including yourself, should have a vision of where they want to get to by the end of the year, and what needs to happen to ensure that they arrive in the right place.

Encourage your people to own their plans from the moment they finish their onboarding. You can play a role in helping them to create them, and supporting them with putting them into practice, but the plans are theirs. Don't abdicate responsibility to your HR or Training departments, because your team won't feel responsible for the plans, nor will they necessarily be what's most needed. Too few sales teams have personal development plans – this is a simple thing you can put right.

Your team's plans should be living, breathing documents that you review with them at least once a quarter. You could think of your team members as having stock values. Company shares increase in worth as the business grows, but is that happening with them? Do they have more skills? Are those skills more developed? Are they more employable and promotable than they were last year? What's their relative value?

Ideas for team learning

Team meetings are something that you already have on a regular basis. But rather than them being a functional exchange, how about using them to create learning opportunities? Anything that you do internally should have an effect externally, so meetings are the perfect environment for improving people's skills. Here are some ideas for you to think about.

Create a learning circle. You may already incorporate knowledge sharing as part of your team meetings. Perhaps a salesperson talks through a recent success, or someone from Product Development presents their new range. That's fine, but it's a one-way process and it's rare for everyone else in the meeting to get much out of it. It's much more effective if you encourage people to be consciously aware of what they're learning, rather than just listening to what someone is saying.

This is where a learning circle come in. With this, you encourage the person who's presenting to share what the topic means to them personally, and the rest of the team to do the same. For instance, if Sally tells the group about a big sale she's just made and how she did it, ask her to verbalize what she learned from the experience, and your people to consider how they could apply this to their own selling techniques. You can then facilitate a discussion about it. If you have an hour, I suggest 15 minutes for the presentation, 15 minutes for Sally to answer questions, 15 minutes for a group brainstorm to explore the meaning behind it, and 15 minutes to discuss the outcomes. Remember that every piece of learning should lead to an action – what will people do with their knowledge in real life?

Set up a book club. I stole this idea from a colleague of mine who I worked with in the 1990s. He bought his whole team copies of Stephen Covey's *The 7 Habits of Highly Effective People*, and each month they'd discuss a chapter in their team meeting. They talked about what it meant to them and what they'd do differently as a result. Is this something that you could do? Could you choose a book on a relevant topic, such as sales, leadership, negotiation, or personal skills? It doesn't have to be a book; it could be a podcast or online article; it's the idea of learning together that's important.

Have a shares club. This is an activity that I carried out with my sales team in the past. We bought shares in our major customers and created a shares club. Everyone invested £20, and once a month in our team meetings we'd review how the shares were performing. Would we keep them, sell them, or buy more? Maybe we'd even buy shares in other companies in the sector. This helped everyone to develop their business acumen, because they started to understand the factors that influenced the performance of a company. Why did certain shares behave the way they did? And what might happen in the future? This is an engaging way for people to learn, and a nice byproduct of it is that you might even make a bit of money that can go towards the Christmas party or a charity donation.[6]

Create a debating society. One year, for a team event, I paired people up and gave them a work-related topic to debate, such as: 'The merger between x and y companies will end up with y as the strongest.' One of them argued for, and the other against. After they presented their cases to the room, the whole team voted on who they agreed with the most. It was fun, but the main value of it lay in how it encouraged people to listen to one another's arguments. This was particularly the case when they had to promote a point of view that they didn't agree with, such as 'Our competitor is better than us.' It really got them thinking. In an age when public debate is increasingly binary, with people either agreeing or disagreeing rather than having a nuanced discussion, the art of debate is more important than ever.

Learn a new skill together. How about deciding on a new skill that you'll learn together as a team? It could be a language, computer coding, or something else that's completely unrelated to work. There's nothing like stretching people into unfamiliar areas to increase their capacity for new ideas.

It's important to have ways of developing your people that bring them together. You don't have to do the same thing every month – you could mix them around and create some variety. As well as waking up people's minds and sparking ideas, you're encouraging them to take ownership of their learning development. This helps newcomers and – even more so – those who've been in their jobs for a long time.

What about under-performers?

Everything we've talked about so far assumes that your people are performing to a reasonable level and want to improve, but I can't deny that you may have some team members for whom this isn't the case. Of course, if your recruitment and onboarding are of a high standard then you'll have far fewer problem people to deal with than if they weren't, but no system is perfect – sometimes the odd rogue salesperson will slip through the net.

What should you do? I imagine that your organization has its own performance management process for this eventuality, and you should certainly follow it. But beyond that, think about how your onboarding and development programme can give you early warning signs. If someone isn't doing well, and having explored the options, you come to the conclusion that it's because they're either not putting in enough work or are fundamentally unsuited to the role, act without delay. Be clear about your standards and the consequences of not keeping to them.

If the worst comes to the worst and you have to ask someone to leave, having a sound performance management process in place means that it shouldn't be a surprise to them. And if you're ABRing, you won't be worried about having a long vacancy gap.

Career and succession planning

Have you ever had the experience of bumping into someone from a previous organization whom you'd have been glad never to see again? That happened to me once. I was at a sales conference and, while walking through the hotel foyer, was pulled up short by a booming voice behind me. 'Simon! Fancy seeing you here!' With a sinking heart,

I turned around to see the face of an old colleague. It was him – there was no escape now.

'Hi there,' I said, forcing my face into an expression of delighted surprise. 'How're things? I hear you're Regional VP of Sales now. Enjoying the job?'

'It's going brilliantly,' he said with a grin. 'They were so desperate to promote me that I managed to get them to up the package and even increase the car allowance. You probably saw my beauty in the car park?'

'Nice' I said feigning interest.

'Problem is, I'm rushed off my feet. I've got my new job but I'm still covering my old one as well, and all the team are reporting into me. It's been going on for months now.'

'That sounds stressful,' I replied. 'But isn't there anyone in your team who could fill your old role? Surely there's someone who can step up to it.'

'Oh no,' he scoffed. 'None of them is good enough. They're all stuck at a certain level, if you know what I mean. Takes a particular calibre of person, you know.'

There was a silence. 'That's interesting,' I said.

As he sauntered off, I pondered the implications of his statement. It seemed that he hadn't developed anyone in his old team to the point at which they could take on his leadership role, because he didn't see it as his responsibility to develop future leaders. There was no succession plan in place, and no attempt to move anyone forward with their career. His problem was of his own making.

Which leads me to ask: have you thought about who your replacement could be? And if so, what are you doing to prepare them for the job when the time comes? Of course, not everyone wants to be a sales leader, but are you aware of where your people want to go in the future? Their aspirations should form part of their personal development plans, so that their learning is geared towards achieving what they want in the longer term. When you provide opportunities for growth, you're ensuring a legacy you can be proud of.

The art of delegation

Key to people's development is having the opportunity to step up to tasks that are 'above their pay grade.' This is not only of benefit to them, but also to you if it allows you to free up your time in a managed way. Think about what you could delegate, and to whom. It shouldn't just be the things that you don't want to do, but those which support someone's development. Could they attend certain meetings as your representative, for instance? Or assist you with presentations or sales planning?

Delegation is an important skill for a leader to learn, but lots of people don't do it. Much of that is down to wanting to retain control; they buy into the old saying: 'if you want something done properly, do it yourself.' Maybe they even worry that delegating means they're not needed anymore. However, if you delegate correctly, explaining clearly what you want and reviewing it afterwards, your delegatee will almost certainly do a satisfactory job of it. And if your concern is that you're not needed anymore, this is unlikely to be the case (but remember, the long-term aim of leading is to make yourself dispensable). Delegation helps key members of your team, and it helps you; it's that concept most beloved of salespeople – a win/win.

The people leader's role is a crucial one for a sales leader, taking your team from recruitment and onboarding, through their programme of personal development, and onto the next phase of their career. In the next chapter we'll explore a different role – that of the business leader.

Key takeaways

- ▹ The people leader role is pivotal to sales leadership, focusing on recruitment, development, and career progression.

- ▹ Always Be Recruiting (ABR) ensures a continuous pipeline of potential talent, reducing hiring delays and performance gaps.

- ▹ Robust onboarding processes accelerate new hires' readiness and foster long-term retention.

▶ Personal development plans and creative team learning initiatives drive individual growth, engagement, and team cohesion.

▶ Succession planning and delegation empower team members, building a leadership-ready culture and sustaining organizational success.

Chapter 9
The
business
leader

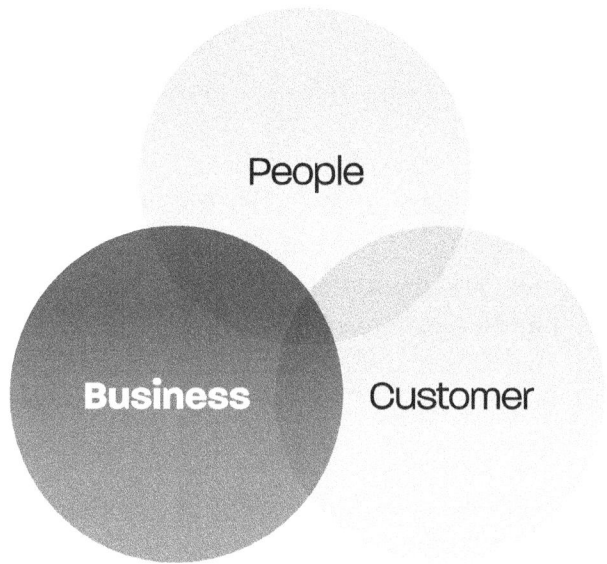

People

Business   Customer

In the previous chapter, we looked at the heart of leadership: building trust, empowering people, and creating a culture where individuals can thrive. But leadership doesn't stop at motivation. It must also deliver results. That's where your role as a Business Leader comes in.

The role of the business leader is one that few sales managers take much pleasure in, partly because it can feel like a chore, and partly because it seems to cater to the needs of the business rather than Sales itself. It's the forecasting, planning, goal setting, monitoring, analysis, and administrative side of your job – the bits that require the production of documentation that people higher up are always asking for. What's more, your sales team probably takes no more interest in it than you do – in fact, less. At best they think of these tasks as distractions, and at worst as actually preventing them from doing a good job.

However, given that you have to fulfil this role whether you like it or not, it's worth taking a fresh look at it. Seen from a leadership perspective, it can fulfil a vital development function for your team if you approach it in a different way. In their book *The Leadership*

Pipeline, authors Ram Charan, Steve Drotter, and Jim Noel dissect the hierarchical levels within every organization.[1] There are individual contributors (salespeople), first-line managers, second-line managers, business unit heads, and finally the CEO. Each level has its own skill set, value set, and time horizon. A salesperson needs selling and problem-solving skills; they value only what they see as directly contributing to their sales success; and they tend to focus on what's immediately ahead of them. However, as a manager your skill set is more leadership-based, being no longer only about yourself but about building your team's success. Your value set therefore involves analysis, planning, and identifying problems (not fixing them); and your time horizon is probably anything up to a year and maybe even longer.

The reason I explain this is because if you're a first-line sales manager who's recently been promoted, you may still be carrying with you the mindset of an individual contributor. However, you now have to step up to a level where you view planning, reporting, and analysis in a different way. Your responsibility is to create success that's sustainable and lasts for longer than the time you spend in your role. You can only do this if you centre your work around achieving the objectives of the organization through the activities of your team, and this requires analysis, planning, and monitoring.

There are three principles of leadership in the business manager role:

1. Sales analysis
2. Sales strategy and planning
3. Execution, monitoring, and reporting

As we explore these principles, you will see how you can apply them to the key areas of forecasting, pipeline planning, and creating a sales process. You'll discover how the 'pen pushing' aspect of your job can – if you carry it out as a true leader – unlock the secrets to developing a high-growth team and sustainable sales success.

Sales analysis

At its core, sales analysis is the practice of monitoring and evaluating sales data to assess the performance of your sales team. By harnessing the power of sales data, you can gain valuable insights into your top-performing products or services, identify areas that require improvement, unearth new market opportunities, and gain a clear understanding of your team's future outlook. When executed properly, sales analysis empowers you to run a more efficient and effective sales team both now and in the future.

Regular sales analysis not only provides you with a deeper understanding of your sales team's performance but also enables you to make better decisions. Sales analysis offers real-time insights into the success of your sales plan, empowering you to make data-driven decisions and refine your approach for optimal results. By leveraging the power of sales data, you can build a more data-driven sales strategy that sets you on the path to unparalleled success.

Choose the right sales analysis method

There are many factors that can influence your sales performance therefore it makes sense that there are a few different types of sales analysis, each of which highlights a particular aspect of the sales process.

Predictive sales analysis. Utilize historical data, current performance, and future variables to forecast potential risks and opportunities, enabling accurate sales forecasting and strategic planning.

Sales performance analysis. Evaluate sales team performance and the effectiveness of your sales strategy by comparing actual results with expected outcomes. Use this analysis to optimize your sales process, boost win rates, and accelerate revenue growth.

Pipeline analysis. Examine the stages prospects go through before converting, providing your team with valuable context to shorten sales cycles and close more deals.

Sales trend analysis. Monitor sales patterns across products, customers, and geographies to track progress towards sales goals and gain valuable forecasting insights.

Product sales analysis. Identify the impact of various products on your bottom line, understand customer demographics, and determine the popularity of different offerings.

Market research. Conduct customer surveys, competitor research, and analyze sales statistics to gain a comprehensive understanding of customer needs and improve sales effectiveness.

The key is to make sure you know what question your analysis is trying to answer. What are you seeking to uncover with your analysis? Determine the relevant metrics and Key Performance Indicators (KPIs) that will provide you with the necessary data to acquire, track, and measure the desired information. Additionally, establish consistent time frames for data collection, such as weekly, monthly, quarterly, or yearly, to ensure meaningful and reliable analysis.

Use your data in the right way

It's likely that you have a lot of information about how your sales team is performing. It might come from your Customer Relationship Management (CRM) system or from other mechanisms that you've developed over the years, but whatever the source, there are almost certainly plenty of numbers to analyze. Because of this abundance of data, it can be helpful to understand that there are two main types of measures to focus on when you're analyzing how well your team is doing.

- ▷ Lag indicators, or results: these are your sales figures, such as the number of units sold, or the revenue achieved.

- ▷ Lead indicators, or inputs: these are what have contributed to your results, such as the number of calls your people have made or the time they've taken to close deals.

When you look at your data in this this way you can see that, while the lag indicators are an important measure of success, you can't do anything about them except to learn from them for next time. It's the lead indicators that contain the richest goldmine of information, because they're the *causes* of your end results. If you use them to tell you what's working and what's not, you can have a direct impact on your sales.

One client I worked with identified that most of the successful deals in his organization involved liaising with three distinct customer stakeholders in specific job functions and with roles within the decision process. This lead indicator told him that if his salespeople didn't bring those three people on board every time, they'd be vulnerable to losing the sale. It became a principle that the whole team adopted, and it was only possible because my client had captured the data that allowed him to analyze the factors leading to predictable success.

Naturally the lead indicators that you choose to focus on will depend on your own sales cycle and business sector. Some sales managers analyze the number of calls or meetings that their people carry out, others look at areas such as pipeline cover. For instance, if you have an overall target of £1 million, you might see from your lead indicators that you need a pipeline of £3 million. Having this in place would put you in a strong position, although it's not a guarantee of success.

So far, so good. But the problem arises when a phenomenon once described by economist Charles Goodhart arises: 'Any observed statistical regularity will tend to collapse once pressure is placed upon it for control purposes.' Often known as Goodhart's Law, what this tells us is that when a lead indicator becomes a target it ceases to become effective.

Suppose your top five salespeople routinely carry out 12 customer meetings a week. 'Aha,' you think. 'This is clearly what everyone should be doing. I'm going to make sure all my team books at least 12 meetings a week.' At first glance this makes sense but think for a moment. By doing this you'd be transforming the lead indicator of 12 meetings a week into a target. Your salespeople might then arrange 12 meetings a week so that they can be seen to be hitting it, but they won't necessarily be the right meetings. Or it might be that some salespeople can smash their targets by having two meetings a week and others need 20. The point is that when you turn a measure into a goal you take away the value of that measure, because fulfilling it becomes an activity in its own right. Now it might be that if you have a salesperson who's struggling to make sales and it turns out that they're only arranging three customer meetings a week, there may be a connection between that and their results. However, you'll only find out by exploring the reasons with them and coaching them around any issues you uncover, not by automatically giving them the target of setting up more meetings.

So, numbers are important, but only as a tool for enabling conversations which reveal the real reasons for problems (and successes). When you spend time on the quality of how your team is working, rather than only on the quantitative aspects, you're in a far better position to improve their performance and create a sustainable pattern of selling. As another law around data says (this time Pearson's Law): 'When performance is measured, performance improves. When performance is measured and reported back, the rate of improvement accelerates.' Capturing and analyzing data is fundamental to learning how to sell better, but only if you understand what good data is and how to use it in a constructive way.

Collect accurate data

Data should give you a clear insight into what's going on, which should then lead you to make the right decisions about how to act. That's why the quality of your data is so important. However, I'm not convinced that sales managers always understand how easily the data they're working with can be corrupted by poor input. So much data isn't useful because it's not reflective of what's really going on, which means that it can't add value to your analysis or help your people to sell more.

The main issue with accurate data collection is that most salespeople see it as a bit of a waste of time; understandably, they'd rather spend their precious hours with customers than plugging figures into a laptop. There's even a chance that they might view it as making their work more difficult. For instance, someone might identify a new customer who's come onto the market, but they know that if they enter the opportunity into the system, various unwelcome outcomes could ensue. For a start, the spotlight is now on them to make the most of this moment. They can foresee all sorts of questions about how they're progressing with it, and the disappointment on their manager's face if they fail to land a meeting. They don't feel ready for that level of exposure yet. Even worse, another member of their team might spot the opportunity and muscle in on it themselves. No, much better to sit on it for now and only enter it into the system when they're sure they can make some headway with it. This renders the data in the system incomplete.

Although data is made up of hard numbers, it's actually full of emotion. If people enter opportunities into their CRM systems only when they feel comfortable that they're likely to materialize, it's because they don't want to open themselves up to being judged or criticized. Or, when they'd rather not follow the demands of a system because they prefer to do things their own way, it's because they value their independence. It's important to recognize this, and to create an atmosphere of psychological safety in which everyone feels secure enough to input what's real rather than what they want you to know.

It's a good idea to have simplicity around data. I've seen sales managers who ask their teams to capture multiple data points that are rarely used. If you can't foresee a purpose for certain types of information, it's best to minimize it so that you're left with the least amount of data that will give you the greatest return. I also encourage people to create a discipline around data capture, because it's much easier to keep on top of it regularly than to tackle an enormous backlog. It also prevents inaccuracies. For instance, if it's 2nd July today and someone closed a deal on 30th June but hasn't yet updated the system, the deal will show as open. That makes it hard for you to know what's going on.

To solve this problem, some organizations send out error and discrepancy reports to prompt salespeople to update their systems. While this might provide a quick fix it doesn't help them to understand why accuracy is important in the first place. I encourage you to gather your team together and go through the report with them, looking at why the errors occur. The reason for doing it as a group is twofold: people are more likely to stop making mistakes if they commit to it in front of their peers, and it helps you to understand if there are general patterns of behaviour that are driving the discrepancies.

An example of such a behaviour is this. Many salespeople enter the predicted close dates for their deals as being at the end of the quarter, in the hope that they'll come good and no-one will scrutinize them too much in the meanwhile. So, when you go through the report and see a lot of deals closing at this time, it should be a warning sign. It might also be the case that some of your people do this more than others. Why is that? Is it because they're not sure about the close date and don't know what else to put? Is it because they're trying to game the system? Or something else? There may be a development need not only in the area of accurate data entry but also in how to judge whether a deal will progress. The same goes for when someone's close dates keep slipping. What's the reason? Is it because they need help with certain aspects of selling? Or with predicting how long a sales cycle is? There are insights that emerge when you go through the numbers with people, and that gives the opportunity for learning at the same time.

In some cases, you might find that many of the deals you have in your system contain made-up dates and details which render them almost useless for analysis. This is not a good situation, but it's far better to know it and have a plan for solving it than to live in blissful ignorance. As long as your team members understand that the data is there for their benefit – to enable them to see where they could perform better – and that you're not looking at it to catch them out but to help them, they will come on board.

Sales analysis as a fundamental practice empowers your sales team to unlock its true potential. By delving into sales data, understanding customer behaviour, and making data-driven decisions, you can transform your sales process and achieve unparalleled success. Better data quality leads to better business planning. Not only improving individual performance and sales effectiveness but helping you plan strategically to maximize the customer base that you are responsible for.

Sales strategy and planning

In the realm of sales leadership, the ability to create, execute, and adjust a robust sales strategy is foundational to success. This aspect of your role as a business leader focuses on the critical elements of strategic planning, resource allocation, and process optimization that drive sustainable sales performance. In the previous section on Sales Analysis, we explored how data insights help guide decisions. Here, we build upon those insights to create strategic sales plans, map territories effectively, and establish a sales process that ensures consistency, accountability, and success. Each of these elements forms a pillar of your toolkit, ensuring that your sales teams are not just aiming in the right direction but are also equipped with a clear path to success.

Strategic sales planning

Sales strategy is the 'why' behind your sales team's activities – the overarching goals and direction that guide all efforts. It involves understanding market conditions, setting high-level objectives, aligning with broader business goals, and determining how to achieve them. At its core, strategic sales planning involves creating a roadmap that directs the team toward achieving revenue targets and business growth.

To craft an effective sales strategy, you must begin by defining clear, actionable, and measurable objectives. These objectives should align with the company's overall business strategy and consider both internal capabilities and external market dynamics. Your strategy must answer critical questions like: What are we trying to achieve? What markets will we focus on? How will we differentiate ourselves from the competition?

Alignment between sales and marketing is crucial in achieving strategic objectives. It's important that you work closely with marketing teams to ensure that messaging, targeting, and lead-generation efforts are cohesive and consistent. A misalignment between these two functions can lead to wasted resources and missed opportunities. By setting shared goals and regular touchpoints for communication, you can ensure a unified approach that drives your sales strategy forward.

One of my clients, a mid-sized technology firm, initially struggled with misalignment between their sales and marketing teams, leading to inconsistent messaging and lost opportunities. After conducting a comprehensive strategy session involving both teams, we developed a unified plan that aligned their efforts toward a common goal: increasing lead conversion rates by 25%. By setting shared KPIs and holding regular alignment meetings, the teams began to work cohesively, resulting in a significant improvement in both lead quality and conversion rates. This transformation not only boosted morale but also created a culture of collaboration, where both sales and marketing saw themselves as partners driving growth.

An essential step in developing a strategic sales plan is to conduct a thorough SWOT analysis (Strengths, Weaknesses, Opportunities,

Threats). This analysis provides a framework for understanding where your team stands and where it needs to focus its efforts. For example, if your team's strength lies in a particular industry vertical, your strategy should leverage this advantage while addressing potential weaknesses. Market research is another vital tool, allowing you to identify emerging trends, potential competitors, and new customer needs.

Through your analysis and planning you can establish SMART goals (Specific, Measurable, Achievable, Relevant, Time-Bound) to provide clarity and direction. These goals should be broken down into actionable steps that are aligned with the overall strategy, ensuring that every member of your sales team understands their role in achieving them. For instance, a SMART goal could be increasing market share by 10% within the next year in a specific region, supported by a detailed action plan.

It's vital that your team is spending its time with as many of the right customers as possible. For that to happen, you have to know what your ideal customer looks like. Can you define them? What is it about them that makes them ideal? Why might they buy what you sell? Can you identify who they are? And how can you best engage with them? This involves you analyzing your customer base, so that you can segment it and direct your salespeople's efforts accordingly.

Territory planning

Territory planning is the 'what' – the specific goals and resource allocation decisions that translate the sales strategy into actionable steps. It involves defining territories, setting quotas, and ensuring that sales efforts are appropriately focused and resourced. Effective territory planning can maximize sales coverage, minimize conflicts, and optimize team performance.

Sales territories should be designed based on potential market opportunity, customer demographics, and sales team capacity. An effective territory plan minimizes overlap and ensures that every customer and potential customer has adequate coverage. You should consider factors like geographic location, industry segments, and account size when defining territories.

Once territories are defined, you need to establish quotas and goals that are both challenging and achievable. These quotas should reflect the potential of each territory and consider the strengths and weaknesses of the salespeople assigned to them. Here are some practical considerations:

▷ **Quota setting based on market potential:** Use market data to set quotas that are reflective of the opportunity within a territory. For instance, a high-growth market may justify more aggressive targets than a more saturated one.

▷ **Incorporating historical performance:** Review past performance data to set realistic quotas. This can help in avoiding unrealistic expectations and in motivating the team by setting attainable, yet challenging goals.

▷ **Customizing quotas for individual salespeople:** Tailor quotas to the capabilities and experience levels of individual salespeople. A newly hired rep may have different targets compared to a seasoned salesperson.

▷ **Regular review and adjustment:** Quotas are not set in stone. Regularly reviewing and adjusting quotas based on performance and market changes is crucial. This ensures that your team remains agile and responsive to market dynamics.

Territory planning is not just about setting boundaries; it's about resource allocation. You must ensure that the right resources – such as time, personnel, and tools – are allocated to each territory based on its potential and the team's capacity. Regular reviews of territory performance can help in reallocating resources as needed to ensure continued growth and success.

An example of this was one of my very first clients that initially assigned territories based solely on geography, leading to uneven workloads and missed opportunities. After a detailed analysis of market potential and the strengths of each salesperson, we restructured the territories to align more closely with sales potential rather than geographic boundaries. This strategic shift resulted in a 30% increase in sales productivity and a more balanced workload across the team.

A well-defined territory plan also builds accountability within your team. Regularly review performance against quotas and provide feedback and support where necessary. This is where your leadership skills in coaching, mentoring, and motivating come into play – ensuring that each team member feels ownership of their territory and is motivated to achieve their goals.

Sales process

The sales process represents the 'how' – the systematic approach that sales teams follow to convert leads into customers. A robust sales process is essential for maintaining consistency, identifying best practices, and driving continuous improvement.

In Chapter 5 we explored the power of developing and following processes, and here I'm relating this to your data. If, through analyzing your figures, you can learn what's created success in the past, you can then calculate what will promote it going forward. Consistency leads to predictability: *when your people do x, you'll probably achieve outcome y*. Even if you're consistently wrong it's better than acting randomly, because consistency makes the reasons for the wrongness easier to identify and correct.

Key to this is focusing most of your attention on lead, rather than lag, indicators. It's easy to see the results that someone's gained, but what about the actions they took to achieve them? If you know what their inputs are you're in a good position to predict what the outcomes will be, as opposed to waiting for the outcome and then working out whether they should have done something different in the first place.

A good analogy for this is sport. If you've won a competition, that's great. But can you repeat your success next time? If you don't have a consistent process for how you achieved it, such as the specific ways you trained and performed, you won't know. You might just have been lucky; you could have benefited from a new diet regime; or it may have been the extra gym sessions that benefited you. Whatever it was, if it was random you'll not learn why.

A dedication to processes can be difficult to instil in Sales, because salespeople often like to think of selling as being a dark art – you can't pin down how it's done. But can you imagine if all departments in an organization worked in the same way? If Finance's attitude to data discipline was, 'It will do', or if Payroll was satisfied with hitting only 92% of its accuracy targets? Salespeople often claim that their role is too complicated and nuanced for a systematic process, but I don't believe it is. If you can create a process for launching a rocket into space that can be replicated and learned from, you can do the same with selling.

Nor does following a process have to erase salespeople's autonomy, which, as we know, is a key factor in their motivation. Helpful processes propel people rather than constricting them. There's no need for sales teams to work in a robotic way just because they're following a system – there's plenty of room for individuality in the way they carry out their work. It's similar to a football team, which has a structure and process to work to, but still allows for individual flair to shine through.

Success doesn't happen on its own – you have to lay a careful path to it, and this is where having a sales process comes in. This maps out what happens in your team's customer engagement journey, from first identifying an opportunity through to closing a deal. Once you have your process you need to work out how you will execute it, and this is where many sales teams come unstuck because they're a bit vague about what they plan to do. The more specific you can be about what you expect to be done and when, the easier it will be for your people to follow, and for you to see when your system is working and when it's not.

Creating a sales process is something that I could write a separate book about so I don't propose to go through every element of it here, but I will highlight the main aspects in which you can bring a leadership approach to bear.

Base your sales process on how your customers buy

In his 1989 book *Major Account Sales Strategy*,[2] sales consultant and academic Neil Rackham introduced the concept of the buying process. He saw it as being made up of six stages:

1. Recognition of need

2. Evaluation of options

3. Resolution of concerns

4. Decision

5. Implementation

6. Changes over time

The idea behind it is that the first thing anyone does when they're thinking about buying something is to recognize that they have a problem that needs solving. They look at the options for doing this, which could involve talking to different suppliers, and weigh them up. Which is best? Does it meet all of their needs? If there are gaps, what are they? They then resolve any issues or concerns and make a decision.

This is a top-level view of the buying process, and your sales process should map neatly onto how customers in your own sector buy. What should your team being doing at the various stages of the customer buying cycle, to take customers from initial interest to closure? And how does that fit with what those customers want? There should be clarity about when one stage finishes and the next stage begins, and everyone should follow it systematically. That might sound prescriptive, but they don't have to carry out every step. There may be occasions on which a particular activity isn't relevant, or when a salesperson needs to do something different. But in most cases these are the steps that they should be taking. If your team does all the right things at the right times, they'll have a better chance of success than if they pick and choose what to do when they feel like it.

For instance, if a salesperson discovers that a lead is interested in a product demonstration, they might jump into doing it without qualifying them first. It's the right thing to do but the wrong time to do it. Before going any further, they should find out why the lead is interested. What's their need? How serious is it? And are they the decision-maker or are there other people who the salesperson should also engage with? If they don't discover this, they might assume that the person they have contact with is in a position to make a decision by a certain date, and only when that date draws near do they discover that there are a host of other people involved. This isn't an efficient or effective way to run a sales process.

By spending quality time on forecasting and pipeline conversations with your team (we'll look at this in the next section), you'll gain a sense of what they're actually doing at each stage of the system, rather than what you might think is going on. In this way your sales process isn't a theoretical analysis of what you assume it should be, but a model of what your best salespeople are doing in reality. If their actions are repeatable, you can use them as lead indicators and build them into the system. It all works together.

Execution, monitoring, and reporting

All the analysis and planning means nothing unless we act upon it. There are some fundamental aspects of the business leader role that if done well will directly support the execution of your plans and help ensure you and your team's success. These are:

- Forecasting
- Pipeline management
- Reviewing progress and reporting

My guess is that you probably view these activities as a bit of a drain on your time, administrative tasks not necessarily helpful for improving your sales. However, I hope you'll see that if you take a leadership approach to them, with coaching and planning at its core, they can be the foundations of solid sales growth.

A leadership approach to forecasting

There's an expression you may have heard: 'Weighing the pig doesn't make it fatter.' So how does this apply in Sales? In almost every organization there's a procedure that takes place at the end of the week, and if you listen carefully, you can probably hear it happening. Laptops are switched on, spreadsheets are opened, and salespeople log into their CRM systems. This is the preparation for the regular forecast meeting. Beads of sweat roll down the foreheads of salespeople as they stare their figures in the face. They examine what they've closed already, look at what they have in their pipeline, and cross their fingers that with a fair wind and a bit of luck these deals will close in time to include in their forecast. Although it might not seem like it, this is the sound of pigs being weighed.

Some of these people will be able to relax; they've achieved or over-achieved their quota and so the weekly group meeting will be a pushover. Others, who are worried about how their numbers will look, mentally rehearse their justifications. Across these two groups, some are optimists who throw in a few deals that have little chance of closing, and others are pessimists who hold back. Whatever their state of mind, few will close their laptops at the end of the call with anything other than a sense of relief that it's over for another week.

This needs to change for two reasons.

It's not an accurate way of creating a forecast

Research from CSO Insights shows that forecast accuracy has been consistently around the 47% level for the past few years, meaning fewer than half of the predictions that sales managers present to their seniors hold true in reality. In addition, a Gartner study revealed that more than half of sales leaders lack confidence in their organizations forecasting accuracy, often due to poor pipeline visibility and ineffective processes that increase the likelihood of errors.[3] These statistics highlight the widespread issues in forecasting, where the odds are often worse than flipping a coin, yet the stakes for businesses remain high.

And yet accurate forecasts are incredibly important to a business. Forecasts dictate manufacturing capacity and service level planning, and also how much the company can afford to invest in its people and equipment. They're reported to shareholders and stakeholders, which makes them a marker of credibility and professionalism. Imagine if an organization had no way of predicting what it was going to sell over the coming months – it would limp from week to week, handling one crisis after another until it imploded under the weight of its own chaos. This is what forecasting is supposed to prevent.

It adds no value to salespeople

I can guarantee that if I was to ask any salesperson, in any organization, in any country, what they thought of their regular forecast call, they'd tell me that it was a waste of their time. That's because most forecasting meetings are a one-way street. The sales manager asks each person in turn for their numbers. What's changed from last week? Why has it changed? Do they have anything else to add? Then they move to the next one. At the end of the call, has anyone learned anything? Have they gained any insights that will help them to sell more effectively? Are they thinking about anything other than what they're going to do once the meeting is over? I think not.

Most salespeople see forecasting as pointless because they gain nothing from the process for themselves – it's all for their manager. The individual salespeople don't understand why forecasting is important for the business, or what the implications are of inaccurate forecasting. Nor do they always have a full appreciation of what it does to their own reputation if they regularly over or under perform compared with their forecasts.

Anything you do internally with a salesperson should be seeking to add value for them externally. So, if you have a forecasting meeting, it should have an impact on how they sell. If your conversation doesn't enable them to become more effective and efficient with customers, it's a good idea to ask yourself why you're having it. ·

There is a better way

In almost every organization I've worked with, forecasting is carried out as a group activity. To the sales managers it seems like an effective way of doing it because they're able to gather all the figures they need in an hour, but in reality it takes a lot longer than that when you consider the preparation that salespeople put into it. The managers also assume that by doing it as a group their people can learn from one another, but again, the reality is that most of them gain nothing from it. Salespeople think as individuals – they're only really interested in themselves.

I remember talking this through with one sales manager who strongly disagreed with me that the group approach was ineffective. She thought that her team got a lot out of hearing what their colleagues had to say about their numbers. So, I said to her, 'When you were a salesperson, how interested were you in what your colleagues were saying in those calls?' She went quiet. 'Well, not much,' she replied. 'To be honest, in the lead-up to my turn I was only thinking about what I was going to say, and afterwards I'd just check my emails.' This is common, and while it may seem as if it's time-efficient for you to get everyone together, in fact it's far more beneficial if you carry out forecasting as a series of one-to-one conversations. There are a couple of benefits to this.

You can incorporate a coaching element so that people learn

Instead of forecasting being a reporting exercise, you can turn it into a coaching conversation so that your people understand the reasons for their numbers. This is most effective as a one-to-one, because it's private and so likely to encourage an honest exchange. You can work with the salesperson to identify which sales are vulnerable to being lost, and what help they need from you to get them over the line. Remember the GROW coaching framework that we went through before? Your conversation could be structured something like this.

G: *The goal for the session. To look at their deals, agree which ones are going to close, and what they plan to do about the ones that might not.*

R: *The current situation. Explore the deals that are on the table. What's happening with this one? And that one? Where are the risks?*

O: *The options. What could they do about the areas of vulnerability? How can they improve the chances of closing an Upside or Best-Case opportunity?*

W: *The way forward. What action will they take? And by when? Do they need any help from you?*

In this way, your forecasting meeting becomes more of a qualitative coaching and engagement session than a numbers-based, quantitative one. Of course, you need the numbers as an outcome, but that shouldn't be the only result you achieve. You're helping your people to look at where they're struggling and to talk things through with you, so that they can ask for help if they need it. And just as importantly, they go away with a concrete set of actions.

You can use it as an opportunity to understand the figures

One of the reasons Sales VPs only stay in their jobs for an average of 18 months is because they commit to over-optimistic forecasts and don't achieve them. So not only do they fail on their numbers, but they also look incompetent at forecasting at the same time. It's no better if they come in massively over their forecast either because that can cause serious problems for the business.

Having proper conversations with your salespeople, in which they feel comfortable enough to be honest about their numbers, is central to you creating accurate forecasts. This should always be what you want to achieve, and you can only do it by understanding what stage all the opportunities are at and how they're going to close. When you have clarity around individual deals you can identify risks and put plans in place to deal with them.

While forecasting accuracy is crucial, its effectiveness relies heavily on understanding the quality and health of the pipeline. Without clarity on where each opportunity stands, it becomes nearly impossible to predict outcomes accurately. This is where pipeline management comes in, providing visibility and structure to sales efforts. According to Matthew Dixon's research in *The Jolt Effect*, between 40 to 60% of all deals result in no decision due to customer indecision.[4] By properly managing the pipeline and identifying at-risk deals, you can prevent opportunities from stalling and take proactive steps to drive them to closure.

A leadership approach to pipeline management

Pipeline planning is an activity that many sales managers find it hard to pay enough attention to, and this has a detrimental effect on their long-term sales. Remember as a leader you want to be focusing on sustainable sales growth, not just to hitting this quarter's targets, and so it follows that to be an effective sales leader a healthy pipeline is one of your key priorities.

There are a couple of reasons why you might not be giving enough focus to your pipeline. The first is that forecasting always seems to take precedence over pipeline planning. Forecasting falls into the top left quadrant (urgent and important) of the Eisenhower Matrix that we talked about in Chapter 5, because there's always a short-term deadline attached to it. That's why it tends to be carried out before pipeline planning, which sits in the top right quadrant (non-urgent and important). However, if you cast your mind back to that chapter, you'll recall that 'non-urgent and important' is where leaders are made – it's the top right quadrant that you want to be paying most attention to.

The other reason for pipeline planning playing the poor relation to forecasting is that you're probably combining your forecasting and pipeline activities together. This is understandable, because they both involve discussions with your salespeople about their immediate and future deals, but if you don't separate them out, you'll be forever giving 80% of your time to forecasting when it should be more like 50%. It sounds obvious, but forecasting is about concrete deals that might close in the current quarter, whereas your pipeline is about less certain deals further ahead. Trying to mix the two together is creating an 'apples and pears' situation.

A better way of pipeline management

As well as carrying out pipeline planning separately to forecasting, it's also a good idea to do it as a series of one-to-one conversations. This has the same benefits as with forecasting, in that it offers opportunities for coaching and also delivers more accurate figures at the end.

To illustrate the benefits of this, let's imagine that you're looking at a year's pipeline and that to sell your services takes an average of six months. Deals that your team are closing in Q1 have been generated the previous year, and you might have one or two that open and close within the current quarter. What most sales managers do in Q1 is to spend their time focusing on the deals that they're going to close soon, which means that as they transition into Q2 the numbers drop off a cliff. They then have to work out the deals that they have further ahead so they can regenerate them and fight to close them. It's as if they're constantly trying to rebuild the pipeline.

Instead of this up and down approach, it's more productive to spend dedicated time discussing your pipeline, so that it's all about future activity. This also benefits your forecasting. If you're in Q2 now and you already know what's in store for Q3 and Q4, when you transition out of Q2 you're aware of which deals are going to close and which have a question mark hanging over them. You'll feel confident in your forecast numbers because you've discussed them with your team members previously, so it's a reliable basis for moving forward.

The beauty of doing it this way is that it actually *benefits* your forecast calls by making them more efficient. When you have your forecast calls, you're then only looking at discrepancies or challenges, and you can spend more time talking with the individual salespeople about what they can do about them. A coaching conversation about pipeline planning could go something like this.

G: *The goal for the session. To make sure the pipeline is healthy and sufficient for the year ahead.*

R: *The current situation. Discuss both the prospecting and early-stage opportunities, and what your salesperson is doing to move them forward. This is important, because any action they take now will have a greater influence than if they leave it until later.*

O: *The options. What are they doing to build their pipeline? This could be cold calling, working with Marketing, or anything else that's relevant. And how are they progressing their marketing qualified leads?*

W: *The way forward. What action will they take? And by when? Do they need any help from you?*

Pipeline health is about more than just size or volume; it's about balance and distribution. A well-managed pipeline should reflect a range of opportunities at different stages of the sales process, ensuring that you're not overly reliant on early-stage deals or a single large opportunity. For example, even if your pipeline shows significant cover, it's a red flag if the majority of your deals are stuck in the early discovery phase or concentrated in just one high-value account. This kind of imbalance leaves you vulnerable – if the big deal falls through or stalls, your ability to hit target collapses. True pipeline health requires diversity in deal size, customer segments, and sales stages, allowing you to mitigate risk and maintain steady progress toward your goals. With this in mind, it's critical to regularly review both the volume and the composition of your pipeline to ensure that it's aligned with your overall sales strategy and capable of delivering sustained results.

Reviewing progress and reporting

Let's imagine you're thinking of joining a gym to improve your fitness. You may already be regular gym-goers, but picture yourself just starting out. Which approach yields better, more sustainable results: going sporadically, doing random exercises with no clear goal, and putting it off for other activities – or maintaining a consistent routine, showing up at regular times, following a structured workout plan, and prioritizing it over less important tasks? Clearly, the second approach delivers superior results. Over time, you get stronger, fitter, and more efficient with the same or even less effort. The same principle applies to your sales leadership – consistency is key to success.

Your operating system

Your operating system is the cadence of meetings and reviews that you set up to ensure everything is on track. It's a repeatable process that becomes more effective over time, allowing you to identify areas of improvement, adjust your approach, and optimize results. Regular forecast meetings, pipeline reviews, and other key discussions should be scheduled with precision and purpose, forming the backbone of your operating system.

Just as regular gym workouts lead to better fitness, a consistent operating system in your sales leadership ensures that you're always moving toward your goals. Research from MIT Sloan highlights that employees with consistent engagement – those who apply regular effort in their roles – perform better than those whose effort fluctuates.[5] Consistency provides clarity and predictability, creating a stable environment where both you and your team can thrive.

Inconsistent leadership, on the other hand, leads to confusion and frustration. When meetings or reviews are scheduled sporadically, the team lacks direction, and performance falters. A regular cadence of forecast and pipeline review meetings ensures that progress is continuously monitored, opportunities are identified early, and challenges are addressed before they become bigger problems. This is the kind of rhythm that drives sustained success.

Elements of a sales operating system

Your operating system revolves around the consistent execution of key meetings and reviews. Each element – whether it's a forecast meeting or a pipeline review – should have a clear purpose, duration, agenda, and inputs like reports or dashboards. This ensures that every session is productive, driving actionable insights and accountability. Let's look at two key examples:

Forecast meeting: In this meeting, you engage with your team to assess the accuracy of forecasts. Consistency is critical here – regular forecast meetings allow you to spot trends, identify risks, and take proactive steps to ensure forecast accuracy. As we discussed earlier, one-on-one coaching during forecast sessions provides a valuable opportunity to delve into individual opportunities and develop a clear picture of the overall pipeline health.

Pipeline review: A well-managed pipeline is essential for predictable sales performance. These reviews should be conducted at a consistent cadence, focusing not only on the size and volume of the pipeline but also on its health – ensuring that there's a good distribution of deals across different stages, sizes, and customer segments. Focus should be on early stage deals as well as prospecting and demand generation activity. By maintaining a regular schedule for pipeline reviews, you create space for continuous improvement and prevent opportunities from stagnating.

Each of these meetings should be optimized for your specific sales cycle. You can adjust the frequency and depth of the meetings based on what drives the best results for your team, but the important thing is to keep the cadence steady.

Your operating system needs to be tuned to the rhythm of your business. If your sales cycle is longer, you may schedule forecast reviews monthly or quarterly. If your cycle is shorter, more frequent meetings may be necessary. The key is to create a rhythm that balances accountability with flexibility. Scheduling regular meetings creates opportunities for course correction and enables you to stay ahead of potential issues.

The value of a regular operating system is that it's easier to track what's working and what's not. Over time, you'll identify patterns and trends in the data, allowing you to continuously optimize the process. Like in the gym analogy, where steady progress enables you to lift heavier weights or complete workouts more efficiently, your sales operating system allows you to achieve more in less time, increasing productivity and performance.

As Stephen Covey famously said, 'What gets scheduled, gets done.' By committing to a regular schedule of meetings, reviews, and check-ins, you ensure that priorities don't slip through the cracks. This consistency also builds trust with your team – they know what to expect and can prepare effectively, leading to more productive and focused conversations. When everyone understands the operating rhythm, you can focus on what matters most: driving results.

Quarterly business reviews (QBR)

As part of your operating system, the quarterly business review (QBR) is a key opportunity to take a step back and assess where you've been and where you're going. While the forecast and pipeline reviews provide regular, short-term updates, the QBR offers a higher-level perspective on the health of your sales team and strategic direction for the next quarter.

The challenge many leaders face with QBRs is finding the right balance between reviewing past performance and looking forward. It's easy to fall into the trap of focusing too much on what has already happened – analyzing past data, wins, and losses in detail. While reflection is important, the true value of the QBR lies in its forward-looking nature. Your aim should be to spend less time reviewing and more time planning, solving challenges, and aligning the team for future success.

QBRs should be treated as collaborative exercises, not as reporting sessions. It's a chance for your salespeople to not only present their performance but to seek input and support from the wider team. The QBR is about collectively charting the path forward, addressing potential obstacles, and identifying where additional resources or adjustments may be needed. A well-run QBR offers a space for honest discussions and solutions-driven thinking.

At its core, the QBR is about creating a focused conversation around the quarterly performance of your sales team. You'll be reviewing KPIs such as win rates, sales cycle lengths, pipeline health, and revenue targets. However, as much as it is a review, the real value comes in what you do with that information. The QBR is the moment where you can turn insights into actions – where you set new goals, reallocate resources, and adjust strategies based on the realities of the market and your team's performance.

Importantly, the QBR is not just a top-down review where sales managers critique performance. Instead, it should be an open forum where salespeople can engage with leadership, raise concerns, and request specific help. Too often, QBRs are seen as merely a way to report upward, but they should also be an opportunity for salesperson to seek guidance and input. The best QBRs encourage dialogue and collaboration between sales leaders and the team, turning data into real plans for success.

An effective QBR balances analysis with forward planning. The structure of your QBR should include the following key components:

Reviewing key metrics: Start by reviewing key metrics such as revenue, win rates, sales cycle lengths, and pipeline health. This reflection on past performance helps identify trends and areas for improvement. However, keep this segment brief – about 20–30% of the meeting's time – focusing on insights rather than just reporting numbers.

Pipeline health check: A thorough review of pipeline health is critical. It's not just about pipeline volume but also the distribution of deals across different stages of the sales process. You don't want all your opportunities stuck in early stages, nor do you want to rely on one large deal that may or may not close. A healthy pipeline reflects a balanced range of deal sizes, customers, and progress across stages. This insight helps ensure that the team is not overly reliant on a single opportunity or stage of the sales process, which can leave you vulnerable.

Forward planning: The majority of the QBR should focus on looking ahead. What actions need to be taken to achieve next quarter's goals? What obstacles could arise, and how can you mitigate them? This is where the real value of the QBR lies – using past performance as a foundation for future planning. This is the time to set new objectives, outline strategic adjustments, and ensure that each salesperson has a clear plan for moving forward.

Collaboration and support: Encourage salespeople to bring forward their challenges and ask for support. The QBR is a chance for team members to seek input from leadership and their peers on how to overcome roadblocks. Whether it's advice on closing specific deals, requests for additional resources, or adjustments to the sales strategy, the QBR should foster open dialogue. Sales leaders must also use this opportunity to provide feedback, guidance, and, where necessary, coach the team on better execution.

Shifting the focus from reporting to collaboration

One of the most common pitfalls of QBRs is treating them as pure reporting exercises, where salespeople simply present what they've done in the last quarter. While a certain amount of review is necessary, this should not be the primary focus. QBRs should be collaborative and solution-oriented. It's about preparing for the future, not rehashing the past.

To foster collaboration, create an environment where your team feels comfortable discussing challenges openly. This means creating space for constructive feedback and ensuring that every QBR ends with clear, actionable steps that align with your sales strategy. Instead of waiting for things to go wrong, the QBR allows you to identify potential issues before they derail progress.

Like the other elements of your operating system, the QBR should have a defined structure. Each meeting should have:

A clear agenda: Set expectations for what will be covered, including metrics, pipeline health, and strategic goals for the next quarter.

Time limits: QBRs can easily run long if not properly managed. Be mindful of the time allocated to reviewing past performance and ensure the bulk of the meeting is spent on forward planning.

Input from team members: Encourage your salespeople to come prepared with data and insights. The more engaged they are in the process, the more valuable the outcomes will be.

Follow-up actions: At the end of each QBR, there should be a set of clearly defined actions and next steps, both for individual salespeople and the team as a whole. These actions should be monitored in the next quarter's QBR to ensure accountability.

The QBR is not just another meeting in your calendar – it's an essential tool for driving accountability, fostering collaboration, and ensuring that your team stays aligned with its goals. By focusing on forward planning and creating a space for honest discussions, you'll unlock the full potential of the QBR process and empower your team to perform at their best.

Managing up and reporting progress

As a sales leader, managing up – keeping senior stakeholders informed and aligned – is crucial for maintaining progress and ensuring that your team's efforts are strategically aligned with broader company goals. This involves more than just formal reporting; it requires proactive communication, transparency, and a clear understanding of what leadership needs to know.

While QBRs, forecast meetings, and pipeline reviews help guide your team, managing up ensures that your leadership stays informed and aligned with what's happening in the field. By engaging proactively and offering both successes and challenges, you create trust and ensure senior leaders are equipped to make informed decisions.

Managing up begins with anticipating the needs of your senior leadership. What do they need to know, and when? It's not just about waiting for formal reviews – it's about regularly providing insights on sales performance, market conditions, and potential obstacles. This proactive approach helps leadership stay ahead of issues and positions you as a reliable, solution-oriented leader.

I remember a piece of advice I was given by a customer, 'Be as quick to come to me with bad news as you would with good news.' I think this is very relevant here. Senior stakeholders need visibility into potential risks early, along with the steps you're taking to mitigate them. Transparency builds trust, and consistent communication keeps everyone aligned.

Aligning sales efforts with organizational goals

Every update you provide should tie back to the company's broader goals. It's not enough to present data – you need to show how your team's efforts contribute to the business's overall success. When reporting progress, frame your updates around how sales performance supports revenue goals, strategic initiatives, and long-term objectives.

This ensures leadership sees the bigger picture and understands how your team is contributing to overall growth. If there are performance gaps, outline the steps you're taking to address them and provide a clear plan to get back on track.

Be solutions-focused. If you're reporting a challenge, offer actionable next steps. Keep your reports visual and easy to digest – dashboards, executive summaries, and high-impact visuals can make your insights more accessible and easier to act on.

Managing up also involves structured reporting, much like how you hold your team accountable through forecast reviews and QBRs. You are held accountable through regular updates on forecast accuracy, pipeline performance, and sales strategy alignment. These reports should focus on the metrics that matter most to the business, such as revenue growth, sales cycles, and conversion rates.

Formal reporting is more than just sharing numbers – it's an opportunity to reinforce your leadership by showing that you are in control of your team's performance. Demonstrating transparency and accountability strengthens the trust between you and senior stakeholders.

Regular alignment meetings with leadership are essential for ensuring both parties remain on track. These meetings provide a space to discuss forecasts, pipeline health, and any necessary strategic adjustments. Use these sessions not only to report but also to seek feedback and collaborate on refining strategies. This should be seen as a two-way dialogue – an opportunity for leadership to provide input while you offer insights on what's working and what needs attention. It's through these conversations that you keep your team's objectives aligned with broader business priorities.

Ultimately, managing up is about building trust. Consistently keep senior leaders informed about both challenges and successes, and tailor your communication to their preferences – whether they prefer data-heavy reports or high-level overviews. By maintaining transparency and anticipating their concerns, you reinforce your role as a trusted leader who can manage not only the team but also the expectations of senior stakeholders.

Effective managing up and reporting progress closes the loop on the business leader role. By proactively engaging senior leaders, aligning your team's work with strategic goals, and fostering trust through transparent communication, you ensure that the efforts of your sales team are recognized and supported at every level. This final step solidifies your leadership, driving alignment between your team's performance and the company's long-term success.

A final thought

As we bring the business leader role to a close, it's important to address a common concern I often hear from clients – 'Are we spending too much time in internal meetings when salespeople should be out with customers?' It's a valid question, and one that every sales leader should ask themselves regularly. Here's my view: every internal meeting or review must directly contribute to improving the team's performance in the field. If it doesn't enhance their efficiency or effectiveness with customers, we should challenge why we're doing it. These meetings and activities aren't just about ticking boxes; they're about driving tangible business results and supporting the growth of both the team and the company.

The operational system we've explored throughout this chapter is designed with that in mind. Salespeople shouldn't feel bogged down by more meetings – quite the opposite. The goal is fewer, more focused meetings with clear objectives, consistent cadence, and measurable outcomes. By maintaining discipline in these key areas – whether it's forecast reviews, pipeline health checks, or QBRs – we create a system that eliminates wasted time, fosters accountability, and ensures every minute spent together is adding real value.

The truth is, today's sales leaders face an overwhelming amount of information and distractions, from hundreds of emails to endless meetings and phone calls. The challenge isn't just managing this chaos, but cutting through it to focus on what really matters: helping the team hit their goals and continuously grow revenue. Short, focused, disciplined meetings allow us to cut down on preparation time and avoid duplication of effort, ensuring that every action drives us toward our core objectives.

I hope this chapter has demonstrated that the role of the business leader is far more than just producing reports and plans. It is, and should be, a fundamental part of leading and developing your team. The systems and structures we've discussed enable you to manage with consistency, guide your team with clarity, and ultimately drive performance that's aligned with the strategic goals of the business.

In the next chapter, we'll explore the final role in the triad: the customer leader, where we'll look at how you can support your team in their customer engagements and maintain alignment between the customer and the broader business.

Key takeaways

- The business leader role focuses on forecasting, planning, analysis, and reporting – tasks critical to strategic and sustainable sales success.

- A leadership approach transforms administrative tasks into opportunities to develop the team and drive meaningful results.

▷ Sales analysis, strategic planning, and execution/monitoring are the three pillars for aligning team efforts with organizational goals.

▷ Maintaining disciplined systems for forecasting, pipeline reviews, and quarterly business reviews (QBRs) ensures consistent performance and accountability.

▷ Internal activities should always enhance customer engagement or sales outcomes; if they don't, their necessity should be questioned.

Chapter 10
The
customer
leader

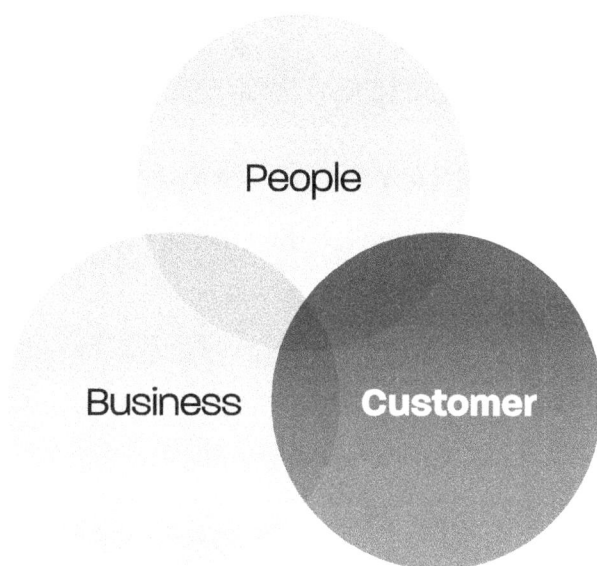

People

Business   **Customer**

So far, we've focused on your internal leadership – how you build your team and drive performance. But leadership also faces outward. The final role in this triad is the customer leader: the person who brings the voice of the customer into your business and ensures your team is aligned to real-world needs and opportunities.

The role of the customer leader is probably the one that's most familiar to you – the part of your job that you feel knowledgeable about and enjoy. Because it encompasses all the various aspects of selling, it speaks to your skill set and makes use of the experience you built up when you were an individual salesperson. Feels pretty good, doesn't it?

And yet the warm glow that surrounds the customer role can also be your downfall as a leader. Left unchecked, it distracts you from keeping your hand on the tiller – guiding and developing your team – and encourages you to jump in as a fixer and problem-solver when things go off track. Is one of your people finding it tricky to finalize a sale? Pick up the phone and close it yourself! Are they caving into pressure from a customer on margin? You've handled that a hundred times before – just tell the salesperson what to say and it's sorted! When sales is in your blood it's tempting to have a 'DIY' approach and take over, which is why we'll explore what *not* to do as a customer leader before we move on to how to carry out the role as a leader.

What not to do as a customer leader

There are three hazards that, in my experience, are most likely to trip up the customer leader:

1. An eagerness to close individual deals

2. A propensity to leap into fixing problems

3. An attempt to combine the role of team manager with being a salesperson for selected accounts

'Hmm', you might be thinking. 'Closing deals, solving problems, and keeping my hand in as a salesperson while also managing my team – that doesn't seem so bad, does it? What's wrong with it?' Let's take a look.

Helping to close individual deals

As a leader, your role is not to be a superstar salesperson. You may have been one in the past, but the thrill of the chase should stay there, where it belongs. I've seen many sales managers behave like big game hunters, waiting until their salesperson has flushed out the prey before moving in for the kill themselves. However, this is the wrong way around. As a leader you shouldn't be involved in the back ends of deals, but much earlier on in the process. I'll explain more about that in a moment, but in essence it means that the more time you spend bagging trophies the less time and attention you can give to the strategic aspects of your job, which are far more important.

This can be hard to accept. You may get a bit of an adrenaline buzz or self-esteem boost from playing a crucial part in closing a deal. However, if that's the case, there's something wrong. Remember Chapter 4, when we talked about Maslow's Hierarchy of Needs? If your psychological needs are bound up in your role, you can't do a good job as a leader because you'll forever be using your position to give yourself a sense of emotional satisfaction. Your responsibility isn't to step in and help people make sales because it gives you a warm feeling, it's to create the circumstances in which they can do it for themselves.

Fixing problems

When you see one of your people struggling with a sale, it's tempting to suggest solutions or even to pick up the phone and deal with it yourself. But you need to consider whether it's right to become involved. Every time you solve someone's problem for them, you take away the opportunity for them to learn for themselves; then, the next time a similar issue arises, you have to do it again. Coaching them to resolve their own issues is the solution you should be looking for.

Sometimes when I talk about this with sales leaders, they say to me, 'That's all very well, but we have some customers who expect a senior manager to step into the deal. I can't very well ignore them, can I?' You can't, but you can find out what they're expecting from you. Is it that they want the head honcho to be involved because it makes them feel important? If that's the case, it's your responsibility to explain to them how you do business. It's not appropriate for you to be their contact, because it's not what you're best at. You're there as a point of escalation, if necessary, but not to be involved on a regular basis.

Another reason might be that they don't trust the salesperson to do a good job without you there. In that case, there's probably a development need for your team member. It could be that they don't feel confident enough to deal with certain issues without involving you or assume that they can't make decisions for themselves. Instead of getting involved directly, you can review the situation with them. Why did it happen? And what can they do to deal with it themselves next time? In both cases it's important to address the underlying issue, rather than to automatically step in when asked.

Being caught in a dual role

In some organizations, sales managers have a dual role in which they're a manager of a team but also carry a quota themselves, often for high value clients or deals over a certain level. While this might seem like a reasonable combination, I've never observed it working effectively. What typically happens is that they struggle to carry out either role well, because it's a constant juggling act.

Why is that? Because rarely is it made clear to the manager which role is more important. They have to decide where to allocate their time, and – as you know – sales isn't a job that can be neatly divided into percentages of hours or days of the week. What's more important to that manager: leading and developing their team, or being a salesperson? It can't be both. In practice, because their compensation is linked to achieving their personal quota, and the salesperson role is the one they feel most comfortable with, they put most effort into that. This causes the sales team to feel neglected, because all they really have is an administrator who signs off their annual leave and authorizes expenses, not a leader who's dedicated to helping them succeed.

If you're in this position, you need to take a step back and consider how you divide your time. It's also a good idea to talk to your line manager about it, because the position you're in isn't sustainable. If it's a temporary arrangement, for instance to help you develop your management skills, you should have an end date and a set of criteria for it finishing. And if you're a VP of Sales yourself and have appointed a manager to a dual role, be clear with them about where their priorities lie and what the next steps are. If possible, eliminate the need for combining the jobs in the first place.

Your relationship with your customers

It might seem from what we've covered that you should keep yourself well away from customers, entrusting all contact to your sales team. I'm not saying that you shouldn't have relationships with customers, only that your perspective on those relationships should be different from that of your salespeople. Your role as a sales leader is to see the big picture when it comes to customers. That means:

▹ Supporting your team with their customers

▹ Being a conduit between your organization and your customers

▹ Customer relationship cultivation and strategic growth

One of your primary responsibilities is supporting your team in their customer engagements. This doesn't mean stepping in to do the work for them; it means coaching and developing their skills so they can execute successfully on their own. The goal is to empower your salespeople to take ownership of their customer relationships and perform at their best. By acting as a coach, you provide the structure and guidance they need to develop into more effective and confident professionals.

Supporting your team with their customers

One of the activities you should encourage your people to do is to set their own sales plan each year. That might seem obvious, but in my experience most salespeople tend to set off on their sales journey without thinking about what their destination is and how they're going to reach it. An individual's sales plan should align with your overall sales strategy and support your territory plan. It captures the objectives and targets of the individual and illustrates how they will achieve these.

This is where the 'plan-on-a-page' becomes an essential tool. It provides a straightforward way for salespeople to structure their goals for the year ahead, to think about their customer activities, to anticipate challenges, and maintain focus on their own development. This plan isn't a static document but a dynamic roadmap that guides their customer engagements and helps them stay accountable.

Plan-on-a-page

When it comes to building this plan, there are three levels of goals that your people should set for their plans.

Their aspirational goal: This is personal for them – their 'why.' What would hitting their quota mean for them? Is it to be recognized as a top salesperson, or to earn a certain amount so that they can move house or have a great vacation? Or something else?

Their performance goal: This is the sales quota you set for them, such as a revenue target. If they hit this, they stand a good chance of achieving their aspirational goal. This goal can be broken down by month or quarter.

Their process goals: These are the inputs – the activities that they need to engage in to achieve their performance goal. It might be making a certain number of calls per day or following up on deals that have reached a specific stage. It may include target customers and specific deals. As long as a process goal is helpful and executed well, achieving it should move the person towards their performance goal. And if they achieve their performance goal, they can hopefully smash their aspirational goal.

Often salespeople have performance goals but not process goals, and the aspirational goals are completely overlooked. Imagine an athlete who's training to be the 100 metres sprint Olympic champion. Their aspirational goal is to win a gold medal, and although they can't directly control whether they achieve it, it's what gets them up on a wet Wednesday morning to pound the track. Their performance goal is whatever time they need to win the 100 metres (let's say it's 9.8 seconds). And their process goals are to train in the gym twice a day, adjust their diet in certain ways, and take nutritional supplements. These are the things they can control and which, if done well, will put them in the best position to run the 100 metres in 9.8 seconds. Breaking down annual targets to quarterly goals and actively setting process goals not only help people perform better but can also make them feel better about their work.[1]

Of course, plans don't always go, well, according to plan. That is why it is also important to anticipate obstacles. Just as the athlete may try to take account for injuries or illness, we too must encourage our salespeople to consider potential challenges that might hinder the execution of their plan. Some challenges can be anticipated and planned for. For instance, if you sell into the Retail sector many retail organizations often slow down or temporarily halt major projects in the months leading up to Christmas. This is because the holiday season is a critical period for sales, and the focus shifts to ensuring smooth operations, stock management, and customer service. How does your salesperson's plan reflect this? What other issues might arise – whether sector or customer specific, regional or geographically based, or seasonal? Also, how will the salesperson react if they are tracking behind plan? What contingency can be put in place?

Your contribution to this planning process is to help your people develop their plans and hold them accountable in the execution of them. It's important to see your plans as live, working documents, reviewing them every week or month. They should always contain milestones, and when a milestone is reached it's important to review it. Have your salespeople executed the actions, and did they achieve what they expected? If so, that's great; can they do the same activities next time? If not, what impact might this have further down the line? And what coaching, encouragement, and motivation could you offer to get things back on track? To bring these plans to life, they can be used and referred to during QBRs, forecast meetings, and pipeline reviews and provide an ideal resource for coaching conversations.

Two ways of improving your team's selling skills

We've talked a lot about coaching as a development activity, but there are two other ways to develop your people's selling skills that are often overlooked:

1. Joint meetings

2. Role play

Let's see why they make a difference and how you can put them into practice, especially when you combine them with the power of coaching.

Joint meetings

These are customer meetings which you attend with an individual salesperson, whether it be in person, or virtually. 'But I do this already,' you say. If so, that's great, but I expect that it goes a bit like this. Your salesperson asks if you can attend a meeting to help with a sticky problem; the customer is playing tough with negotiations or asking for an unreasonable discount. You agree, but because it's last-minute you don't have time to talk it through beforehand and have to drive to the customer's office in separate cars. After a hasty conversation in the car park you go in, have the customer meeting, walk back out, and go your separate ways. Maybe you solved the problem or maybe you didn't, but either way there's only a minimal development opportunity for your salesperson involved.

This isn't the sort of joint meeting I'm talking about. First, it's important to understand what it's not, which is you getting involved at the end of a deal or meeting a customer to solve a problem. In fact, your aim shouldn't be to play an active role at all, because the purpose of you being there is to observe your salesperson doing their job so you can see how you can help them to improve.

In fact, joint meetings work best when you build them into a routine, so that you're attending a variety of meetings with all your people and a representative selection of your customers, at different stages of the sales cycle. This will enable you to observe different things going well or badly. You don't just want to be wheeled into sessions that your salespeople have set up for you – the ones they want you to be at. It's a bit like when there's a Royal visit somewhere and it always smells of paint.

This is an overview of how your joint meeting should work, step by step.

1. Make it clear to the salesperson that the purpose isn't to catch them doing something wrong, but to help them improve.

2. See how they prepare for it: what objectives they set (if any), and what they view as being the steps to achieving them.

3. Ask what they would like you to observe – is there something that would be helpful for them? This encourages them to think about their own development.

4. When you arrive at the meeting, clarify to the customer what your role will be, as this avoids them talking directly to you and undermining the authority of the salesperson.

5. Finally, after the meeting is over, carry out an immediate debrief. This allows the salesperson to evaluate themselves and gives you the opportunity to coach and support them around anything they found challenging. That's the reason you're doing the joint meeting: to help them to become better in front of their customers.

I'm often told by sales managers that they don't have time for joint meetings, but if you think like that you have little idea how well your people are carrying out the bread and butter of their jobs. The only metric you have is whether they're hitting their targets, which is a lag indicator – it's too late. You need to know what the inputs are, so you can make a difference early in the process.

Role play

Cast your mind back (if you're old enough) to the early 1990s. Bill Clinton had just been elected US President, shoulder pads were on their way out, and I was a fresh-faced salesperson just started at British Telecom. One day I happened to be visiting the London headquarters when I bumped into Bill Murphy, the Sales Director (the CSO as he would be in today's money). It was a somewhat terrifying experience because he had a reputation for knowing everything about everyone in Sales, and I was about to be proved right. Despite the fact that he ranked four or five levels above me, one of hundreds of salespeople, he greeted me by name and asked what I was up to. What customers was I working with, and how was it going? I explained that I had an important meeting with one of my customers the following day. 'I tell you what,' he replied. 'Why don't we role play your meeting?'

Gulp. This was not what I had in mind, but what an experience it was. It soon became clear that his aim wasn't to catch me out, but to help. In fact, he went on to spring role plays on me and my colleagues multiple times over the course of my career, and I never failed to discover new insights about my selling skills that would benefit me for years to come.

Most people dislike role play. They feel self-conscious, claiming that they'd normally behave differently in real life, or that it's meaningless because it's a false situation. I say, 'Can you imagine a football manager agreeing not to practise penalties because it's not a real match?' The reality is that how we act in a role play is rarely dissimilar to how we'd behave with a customer. It's the next best thing to being in an actual customer meeting, with the opportunity to learn through coaching and observation thrown in.

Role play is also a great way of rehearsing. Shipping magnate Aristotle Onassis, at the time one of the richest people in the world, would often be overheard by his PA rehearsing meetings before he went into them. He never left the encounter to chance. This is so valuable, and something that we rarely do in business. Practise gives your people the opportunity to try out different responses to challenging situations, just like politicians do when they prepare for televised interviews. It also builds muscle memory, so that when they're in a pressured situation they know how they're going to respond. There's a saying that many performers use: 'Don't practise until you get it right. Practise until you can't get it wrong.'

Just a final point about role play and rehearsal: don't try to solve every problem at once. It's better to identify one area for improvement at a time, and not start on the next one until the first is mastered. You can think of it as layering skills one on top of another, which is a much more manageable way for people to learn. It might be, for instance, that someone has difficulty in asking for a commitment from customers. You can talk through the different reasons that the customer might give, and role play how the salesperson could respond. Once you have a few options that you're both happy with, they can rehearse them and then try them out in real life. This might take some time, but it will save you many more wasted hours fixing problems for them again and again – and improve their sales figures as well.

Being a conduit between the customer and the organization

As a sales leader, your role extends beyond just managing your team's customer relationships; you're also a critical link between your customers and the broader organization. During joint meetings with your salespeople, you'll hear firsthand how customers perceive your organization, your sales process, and your overall ease of doing business. These interactions offer invaluable insights into customer needs, concerns, and frustrations – insights that are often not apparent from a distance.

Your role, as a conduit, is to ensure that the voice of the customer is heard internally and acted upon. Customers want simplicity. They want doing business with your organization to be as smooth and frictionless as possible. It is your responsibility to advocate for their needs, remove internal barriers, and align your company's processes with customer expectations.

Advocacy and removing internal obstacles

One of the most critical functions of a customer leader role is to remove the obstacles that slow down or frustrate the customer experience. These obstacles often come in the form of bureaucratic roadblocks – such as extended sign-off processes, deal desks, or cumbersome approval procedures – that delay decision-making and prolong the buying journey. Research from McKinsey has shown that companies with streamlined internal processes are significantly more likely to achieve higher customer satisfaction scores.[2]

The key is to identify where friction exists and advocate internally to eliminate it. By championing the customer's perspective within your organization, you not only improve their experience but also empower your sales team to operate more efficiently. For example, simplifying approval processes or ensuring quicker internal communication between departments can drastically reduce the sales cycle, allowing your team to close deals faster.

When you advocate for process improvements internally, you are also supporting your salespeople. A quicker, more efficient sales process reflects positively on the salesperson, making it easier for them to build stronger relationships with customers and deliver on their promises. The less time spent navigating internal bureaucracy, the more time your team can spend focusing on the customer.

It follows that the more you can remove the need for your salespeople to request signoffs or approvals, the better. If they have to ask you to agree to everything, you become a bottleneck, and that's not good for anyone – least of all your customers. Of course you can't give your team complete free rein, but if you find that you're constantly being asked for the same kind of sign-off it's worth revisiting your systems and processes. They might have been right for yesterday, but are they still fit for today?

Fostering cross-functional collaboration

Effective sales leaders work across departments to ensure that customer feedback is acted upon. Whether it's marketing, product development, or operations, cross-functional collaboration is key to ensuring that customer insights translate into meaningful internal changes. Forrester research has shown that companies with integrated cross-functional collaboration are 2.5 times more likely to improve customer satisfaction and loyalty.[3]

One way to accelerate this collaboration is by inviting other relevant departments to your QBRs. Allowing departments like marketing or product development to hear customer feedback firsthand ensures they better understand the customer's needs and challenges. This creates a more cohesive internal alignment, where all functions can contribute to addressing customer pain points. Furthermore, this direct exposure to customer insights helps teams to align their efforts more effectively with customer-centric strategies, improving not only product and service offerings but also overall customer satisfaction.

In fostering collaboration, you also support your salespeople by ensuring that their efforts to meet customer needs are backed by the entire organization. When sales, marketing, and product teams are aligned, it creates a seamless customer experience that enhances trust and long-term loyalty.

Using customer insights to inform strategy

As a conduit, you are uniquely positioned to gather a wide range of customer insights, from specific product feedback to broader market trends. While individual salespeople may focus on their immediate customers, you can take a wider view – listening to feedback from multiple sources and identifying key themes that can influence broader company strategy.

For example, if you start hearing similar concerns from different customers – whether it's around pricing, product features, or service delivery – it's your responsibility to relay this feedback to the relevant departments. A report by Microsoft found that organizations that leverage customer behaviour to generate insights outperform their peers by 85% in sales growth.[4]

Additionally, customer insights can inform decisions about market positioning, competitive strategy, and even product development. For instance, if customers consistently mention a competitor's strengths, that's valuable information that should be shared with your marketing and product teams to adjust positioning or develop new features. By continuously feeding this information back into the organization, you help ensure that your company remains agile and responsive to market needs.

When sales leaders embrace their role as conduits between the customer and the organization, the benefits are substantial:

▷ **Enhanced customer loyalty:** By addressing customer needs and resolving concerns quickly, you build stronger relationships, which leads to repeat business. Customers appreciate when they feel heard and valued, and this fosters long-term loyalty.

▷ **Improved product development:** The insights you gather from customers can directly influence product development. If customers are asking for specific features or improvements, ensuring that these requests reach the right teams can lead to more competitive products in the market.

▷ **Optimized sales strategies:** By relaying market trends and customer preferences to your internal teams, you help refine sales tactics, making them more effective. For example, if your team understands what's trending in the market, they can better position your offerings and adjust their strategies to meet evolving customer needs.

▷ **Increased sales performance:** When your internal processes align with customer expectations, your sales team will find it easier to close deals, resulting in higher performance. Removing internal roadblocks and facilitating quicker decision-making speeds up the entire sales cycle and enables your team to focus on what really matters – building relationships and driving sales.

As a customer leader, your responsibility goes beyond managing day-to-day customer interactions. You are an advocate, a strategist, and a leader who ensures that your customers' voices are heard and acted upon within your organization. By removing internal obstacles, fostering collaboration, and using customer insights to inform strategy, you play a crucial role in aligning your company's efforts with the needs and expectations of your customers.

In the end, the most successful sales leaders are those who bring customer-centric thinking into the heart of their organization – creating a culture where customer needs are not only understood but also shape the future of the business.

Customer relationship cultivation and strategic growth

I must admit, in some of the leadership roles I've held, I probably didn't spend nearly enough time with customers. Actually, let me qualify that – not enough quality time with customers. If you picture your sales process, it's probably a linear one, starting on the left-hand side with identifying potential opportunities and qualifying, and ending on the right with negotiating and closing individual sales. Too many of my engagements were towards the right-hand side of the process. Coming in with blue lights flashing, hoping to rescue a deal going south or solve an issue that required the extra pips on my shoulder. Too many of us spend our time with customers dealing with emergencies and issues – emergencies that could have been avoided if we had engaged earlier. We all need to swipe left on this.

I think this highlights one of the common challenges sales leaders face: spending too much time on reactive firefighting and not enough on cultivating strategic relationships with customers early on. The role of a sales leader extends beyond simply stepping in when deals are at risk; it's about building deeper, long-term relationships with customers. This requires shifting focus to the left-hand side of the sales process, where you can engage in more meaningful, proactive conversations with customers.

Moving to the left: building strategic relationships

A fundamental shift sales leaders must make is moving away from reactive deal-saving on the right-hand side of the sales process and focusing more on the left-hand side. Engaging with customers early allows for deeper, more strategic conversations about their broader business goals and future challenges, rather than being limited to immediate sales transactions.

It's essential to guide your team to engage with customers before problems arise. By taking this proactive approach, you position your team and organization as partners in the customer's success, rather than just suppliers of products or services. When engaging earlier in the process, you can discuss broader business objectives with customers – understanding where they want to go and how your organization can help them get there. This shift in focus allows you to align the customer's goals with your company's capabilities, building a foundation for long-term strategic growth rather than focusing only on individual deals.

Your role is not just about managing the deal pipeline – it's about cultivating long-term, strategic relationships with high-value customers. While the salesperson handles the day-to-day interactions, you have a crucial role in supporting and strengthening the relationship at a senior level. You should sponsor or co-own relationships with key stakeholders in high-potential or strategic accounts. This means being actively involved in important relationships but not taking over from the salesperson. Your involvement should add strategic value and demonstrate to the customer that your organization is committed to their success at every level.

Another key benefit of your involvement is providing continuity, especially when salespeople change roles or leave the company. When you have an established relationship with key decision-makers, you ensure that the relationship continues to thrive even if there are changes within your team. This level of engagement is critical in maintaining long-term customer loyalty.

Segmentation and strategic account management

Not all customer accounts require the same level of attention, and it's important for you to guide their teams in prioritizing and segmenting customers based on their growth potential. A strategic approach to customer segmentation ensures that the right accounts receive the most attention and resources. By segmenting your customer base into categories such as *key opportunities* (new business potential), *growth accounts* (expansion within existing clients), and *defensive accounts* (those you cannot afford to lose), you can focus your efforts on where they will have the greatest impact.

Your role is to guide your team through this segmentation process and help them build tailored strategies for each category. Encourage the use of strategic account plans for key customers. These plans should detail how the relationship will be nurtured and expanded over time, focusing on long-term objectives rather than immediate transactions. As a leader, you are responsible for ensuring that these plans align with both the customer's and your company's strategic goals.

Representing the organization in the market

Beyond managing relationships with individual customers, you play a broader role in representing the organization in the wider market. Industry leadership at events, conferences, and forums allows sales leaders to build credibility for the organization and foster relationships at a macro level. By being visible in these arenas, you demonstrate thought leadership and reinforce your company's reputation as a trusted partner.

In addition to representing the organization, industry events provide valuable opportunities to gather insights from a broader audience. Listening to feedback on market trends, customer challenges, and competitor strategies allows you to bring fresh insights back to your internal teams. This external perspective helps inform both your sales strategy and broader business decisions, keeping your organization agile and responsive to market changes.

Mitigating risks and ensuring relationship resilience

While building long-term relationships is critical to driving growth, it also comes with risks. Over-reliance on key customers or changes in customer leadership can disrupt these relationships and impact your business. You must ensure that their teams are not overly dependent on a few strategic accounts, while also building resilience into those relationships.

Encourage your team to diversify their focus across multiple accounts to reduce the risk of being vulnerable to changes within one or two key customers. At the same time, staying engaged with multiple stakeholders within a customer's organization helps reduce the risk of losing the relationship if a key contact leaves. This multi-layered approach ensures that relationships remain resilient, even in the face of leadership or structural changes within the customer's business.

Hopefully you're starting to visualize the overlap of the three roles of the people leader, the business leader, and the customer leader, and how they can support each other (also saving you time in the process). As the customer leader you can cross over with the people leader through role play and rehearsals for customer meetings. As the business leader you can overlap with the customer leader through helping your people to set their own sales plans. And as the people leader you can cross over with the business leader through taking a coaching approach to forecasting and pipeline management. The more you bring your three roles together, the more of a confident and effective leader you'll become, and the higher the level of growth in your team you'll achieve.

These three roles – people, business, and customer – aren't separate hats you wear at different times. They overlap. In fact, the best leaders blend them instinctively. It's in focusing on these intersections that your real leadership shows up.

Key takeaways

> ▷ Effective customer leadership focuses on empowering salespeople rather than stepping in to close deals or solve problems.

▶ Building strategic, long-term customer relationships ensures alignment with organizational goals and enhances loyalty.

▶ Salespeople should develop and execute their own sales plans, supported by coaching and structured accountability.

▶ Role plays and joint meetings are powerful tools for improving selling skills and preparing for real-world challenges.

▶ Acting as a conduit between customers and the organization ensures frictionless interactions, informed strategy, and continuous improvement.

What's next?

If you've enjoyed this book, I expect that you'll have identified many things you want to change, whether they be within your mindset, your skillset, or the way you do things. However, whenever we learn a lot in one go it can feel daunting. Remember Warren Buffett's pilot from Chapter 1? Buffett advised him to pick his top five goals and to concentrate only on them until he'd achieved them all; when he'd done that, he could focus on others. There's so much sense in this. When you feel stressed and snowed under, the adrenaline rush you get from running from one emergency to another makes you want to solve every problem in one go, as a series of quick fixes. But as we've explored, all that achieves is a wilting trail of sticking plasters for you to pick up later.

That's why I'm going to go a step further than Buffett (brave, I know) and ask you to pick *only one* thing to change at first. I want you to choose a single cornerstone activity – the thing that if you do it well, will have an impact on the greatest number of other areas you want to improve on. To help you to choose what it is, let's take a step back and look at what we've covered.

First, we explored what the real problem with your sales team is: you (sorry). Everything starts and stops with you, the head of the team. Which means that the key solution to your problems is to build your own leadership skills, the most useful of which is to find ways of developing and growing your people's capabilities. To do this, you need to feel confident that you can take on the task, which is something you can achieve through self-knowledge, self-care, and deciding what kind of leader you want to be. Remember 'Be, Do, Get'? It's the quality of your self-image that's the foundation stone of your shift from manager to leader. Leadership is something you 'be' as well as 'do'.

Next, we looked at how you can develop your team. This involves shifting your focus to the most important 'rocks' in your day and developing systems and processes that are easy to repeat and learn from. It also means learning what really motivates people (and what doesn't) both as individuals and as a group. We also delved into the why and how of coaching. This empowers your team and helps them to feel motivated, because it gives them knowledge that they can transfer from one situation to another. Coaching transforms their performance and saves you time in the long run.

Finally, we explored the three roles of the sales leader: the people leader, the business leader, and the customer leader. As a people leader your responsibility is to recruit, onboard, and train people so that they perform to a high standard right from the start. As a business leader, you have the option of turning a set of bureaucratic exercises into a significant opportunity to develop your people. And as a customer leader, you have the chance to stop fixing people's problems and start taking a strategic approach, through sales planning and building customer relationships.

Your task is to think through these areas, flicking back through the book if you need to. Every time you identify something you could do which would make a significant difference to your leadership ability, note it down. Don't worry for now which you'll focus on first – you're just wanting to generate a list. For instance, your list might look something like this.

- ▷ Start journaling on the way home from work so I can reflect and feel more in control.

- ▷ Get myself a coach.

- ▷ Work out which of my regular tasks currently fit into which boxes of the Eisenhower matrix, and make the necessary changes.

- Write down how much autonomy, competence, and relatedness I offer to my team, and come up with ways to increase them.

- Start coaching people rather than telling them what to do (or doing it for them).

- Learn more about coaching – buy a book or go on a course.

- Start to 'always be recruiting.'

- Change the way I carry out forecasting so that it becomes a coaching opportunity.

- Work out which customers I need to build strategic relationships with and start doing it.

Your list might look very different to this – it doesn't matter. The key thing is that you've identified what will make a difference to *you*. When you have your list, take a moment to work out what *one thing* on it would have the greatest impact. I can't tell you which it is, but you will know. Then – and this is crucial – make a start today. It doesn't matter if it doesn't go well at first, just keep at it because it's only by doing it and learning from it that you'll improve. Soon you'll have the satisfaction of seeing results, which will make you feel more confident. Carry on until you've reached a level of accomplishment that you feel happy with for now, and then – and only then – start on the next action. I can't tell you how satisfying this process is if you discipline yourself to focus on one thing at a time.

Build the right habits

Once you've started working in a different way you'll build new habits, and this makes the change process easier. Our brains are always looking to conserve energy, which is why when something's a habit it becomes less effortful to do. In his book *The Power of Habit*,[1] Charles Duhigg explains his research that 40 to 45% of what we do is habitual, even if it seems that it's a conscious decision at the time. 'It's 12 o'clock so I'll go for lunch,' or 'It's Monday so I need to plan my week.' Creating routines that combine elements of each of your three roles will support your efforts to be an effective leader. In other words, the execution of sales leadership will become second nature.

Being an influential and effective sales leader is one of the most rewarding paths you can take in your career. Issues that previously seemed impossible will seem resolvable, and situations that were stressful will appear simpler. Most importantly of all, you'll create a high-growth team culture that will lead to increased sales. I hope that you feel encouraged to make that choice.

Lead. Inspire. Grow. The transformation begins here.

Notes

The real problem

[1] *Global risks report 2023* (2023) *World Economic Forum*. www.weforum.org/reports/global-risks-report-2023

[2] Hoar, A. (2015). *Death of a (B2B) salesman*, *Forrester*. www.forrester.com/report/Death-Of-A-B2B-Salesman/RES122288

[3] CEB: *The New High Performer Playbook*, Arlington VA, 2012.

[4] Gartner: *5 Ways the Future of B2B Buying Will Rewrite the Rules of Effective Selling*, August 2020.

[5] Gartner: *5 Ways the Future of B2B Buying Will Rewrite the Rules of Effective Selling*, August 2020.

[6] CSO Insights: 2018 *Sales Performance Optimization Study*, March 2018.

[7] The Harris Consulting Group: *Sales Enablement Industry Report 2019*.

[8] Pink, D.H. (2013). *To sell is human: The surprising truth about persuading, convincing, and influencing others*. Edinburgh: Canongate.

[9] Covey, S.R. (2004). *The 7 habits of highly effective people*. New York: Simon & Schuster.

[10] Orlob, C. (2018). *The VP sales' average tenure has shrunk 7 months – here's why*, *Gong*. www.gong.io/blog/vp-sales-average-tenure/#:~:text=The%20VP%20Sales%27%20Job%20Tenure,Months%20–%20This%20Trend%20Explains%20Why&text=The%20VP%20of%20Sales%27%20average,it%27s%20now%20just%2019%20months

[11] Clear, J. (2020). *Warren Buffett's '2 list' strategy: How to maximize your focus and master your priorities*. https://jamesclear.com/buffett-focus

The journey, not the destination

[1] Wiseman, L. (2017). *Multipliers, revised and updated: How the best leaders make everyone smart*. New York: HarperCollins Publishers Inc.

[2] https://hbr.org/2018/03/create-a-growth-culture-not-a-performance-obsessed-one

[3] Dweck, C. (2017). *Mindset – updated edition – changing the way you think to fulfil your potential*. London: Little, Brown Book Group.

[4] www.valuebasedmanagement.net/methods_ulrich_results_based_leadership.html

[5] https://performanceculture.com/the-case-for-the-performance-values-matrix

The secret to confident leadership

[1] Pappas, A., Schrock, W., Samaraweera, M. & Bolander, W. (2023). A competitive path to cohesion: Multilevel effects of competitiveness in the sales force. *Journal of Personal Selling & Sales Management*, 1–19. 10.1080/08853134.2023.2170237

[2] Seligman, M.E.P. & Csikszentmihalyi, M. (2000). Positive psychology: An introduction. *American Psychologist*, 55(1), 5–14. https://doi.org/10.1037/0003–066X.55.1.5
[3] www.gallup.com/cliftonstrengths/en/home.aspx
[4] www.viacharacter.org/character-strengths
[5] Biswas-Diener, R. & Dean, B. (2007). *Positive psychology coaching: Putting the science of happiness to work for your clients.* New Jersey: Wiley.
[6] Sinek, S. (2011). *Start with why: How great leaders inspire everyone to take action.* London: Penguin Books Ltd.
[7] Lencioni, P. (2008) *Five temptations of a CEO: A leadership fable.* San Francisco: Jossey-Bass.
[8] Maltz, M. (2015). *Psycho-cybernetics.* London: Penguin Putnam Inc.
[9] Tang, Y.Y., Hölzel, B.K. & Posner, M.I. (2015). The neuroscience of mindfulness meditation. *Nature Reviews Neuroscience*, 16(4), 213–225.
[10] Alidina, S. (2020). *Mindfulness.* Hoboken: John Wiley & Sons, Inc.

When do I find time for all this?

[1] Don't been too concerned about the monkeys. I don't think that the experiment is actually true, but why let the truth get in the way of a good story? It's a modern-day fable and a great metaphor for how a culture is formed. The story was probably inspired by experiments carried out by G.R. Stephenson, details of which can be found in *Cultural Acquisition of a Specific Learned Response Among Rhesus Monkeys*, and loosely based on the experiments of psychologist Harry Harlow. Now I would be concerned about his monkeys!
[2] Towers Perrin (2006). *Ten steps to creating an engaged workforce: Key European findings.* Towers Perrin HR Services.

Keys to building an engaged team

[1] Mercer (2007). *Exploring the Global Drivers of Employee Engagement*, www.mercer.com/referencecontent.htm?idContent=1281670
[2] *Employee Engagement: A review of current thinking*, by Gemma Robertson-Smith and Carl Markwick. Institute for Employment Studies.
[3] Johnson, M. (2004). *The new rules of engagement: Life-work balance and employee commitment.* The Chartered Institute of Personnel and Development.
[4] Pages 17–20 of the IES report.
[5] https://blog.bestcompaniesgroup.com/blog/disengaged-employees
[6] Page 41 of the IES report.
[7] www.workstars.com/recognition-and-engagement-blog/2020/03/19/why-employees-quit-11-evidence-based-reasons/
[8] www.linkedin.com/pulse/employees-dont-leave-companies-managers-brigette-hyacinth/
[9] Deci, E.L. & Ryan, R.M. (2008). Self-determination theory: A macro theory of human motivation, development, and health. *Canadian Psychology/Psychologie Canadienne*, 49, 182–185.

The power of coaching

[1] Whitmore, J. (2017). *Coaching for performance: The principles and practice of coaching and leadership*. London: Nicholas Brealey Publishing.
[2] CSO Insights, 2016.

The people leader

[1] www.siliconroundabout.org.uk/2017/10/roger-philby-ceo-of-the-chemistry-group-explainsif-you-only-do-one-thing-to-improve-your-hiring-it-should-be-this
[2] Chamine, S. (2012). *Positive intelligence: Why only 20% of teams and individuals achieve their true potential and how you can achieve yours*. Austin: Greenleaf Book Group.
[3] www.forbes.com/sites/jimkeenan/2015/12/05/the-proven-predictor-of-sales-success-few-are-using
[4] www.mckinsey.com/business-functions/marketing-and-sales/our-insights/for-top-sales-force-performance-treat-your-reps-like-customers
[5] CSO Insights, *2017 Sales Enablement Optimization Study*, Miller Heiman Group.
[6] Depending on your sector or company there may be issues relating to insider trading or some other potential conflict of interest. Be mindful of these, but don't just dismiss the idea because it might be hard or not work for you in an obvious way. What could you do to provide the same learning experience instead?

The business leader

[1] Charan, R., Drotter, S., & Noel, J. (2011). *The leadership pipeline: How to build the leadership powered company*. San Francisco: Jossey-Bass.
[2] Rackham, N. (1989). *Major account sales strategy*. New York: McGraw-Hill Education.
[3] Gartner. (2020, February 12). *Gartner says less than 50% of sales leaders and sellers have high confidence in their managers*. Gartner Newsroom. www.gartner.com/en/newsroom/press-releases/2020-02-12-gartner-says-less-than-50--of-sales-leaders-and-selle
[4] Dixon, M., McKenna, T. & Pohlmann, T. (2022, June 14). *Stop losing sales to customer indecision*. Harvard Business Review. https://hbr.org/2022/06/stop-losing-sales-to-customer-indecision
[5] Somers, M. (2023, October 11). *To truly boost productivity, focus on consistent worker engagement*. MIT Sloan School of Management. https://mitsloan.mit.edu/ideas-made-to-matter/to-truly-boost-productivity-focus-consistent-worker-engagement

The customer leader

[1] Van Buggenhout, N., & Ellis, J. (2024, May 14). *The big power of small goals*. PwC. www.pwc.com/gx/en/issues/workforce/big-power-small-goals.html
[2] Schaubroeck, R., Holsztejn Tarczewski, F. & Theunissen, R. (2016, March 3). *Making collaboration across functions a reality*. New York: McKinsey & Company. www.mckinsey.com/capabilities/people-and-organizational-performance/our-insights/making-collaboration-across-functions-a-reality

[3] Keitt, T. (2020, December 2). *The Forrester Wave™: Customer experience strategy consulting practices, Q4 2020*. Forrester. www.forrester.com/report/the-forrester-wave-customer-experience-strategy-consulting-practices-q4-2020/RES156096

[4] Marotta, D. (2023, October 3). *Customer insights: What they are & why they matter*. Hitachi Solutions. https://global.hitachi-solutions.com/blog/what-are-customer-insights/

What's Next?

[1] Duhigg, C. (2013) *The power of habit: Why we do what we do, and how to change*. New York: Random House.

The author

Simon Jackson is a business performance coach and mentor with over 30 years' experience in sales and leadership. He has held senior roles with BT and Vodafone and worked as a senior consultant with Accenture, supporting global brands on leadership development and strategic transformation.

Today, Simon partners with organizations across sectors to develop leadership capabilities and drive sustainable growth. A qualified coach, he gets a buzz out of helping people to shine and believes that when people enjoy what they're good at it leads to great results. Central to that is enabling them to grow as leaders so that they can inspire their teams.

He's fascinated by what drives performance, and by the rituals and behaviours of high-performing people. As a close follower of the NeuroLeadership Institute and the British Psychological Society, he has access to the latest research in neuroscience and social psychology. He also holds qualifications in Business and Personal Coaching from the University of Chester, and is a member of the International Coaching Federation, with Professional Certified Coach (PCC) credentials. He uses all this knowledge to help his clients take the necessary steps to improve their performance and results.

Simon's motto is 'challenge to change', which means that he uses soul-searching questions and direct feedback to enable sales leaders to become better and more focused versions of themselves. If you're interested in talking to him about working with your business, or speaking at your event, you can contact him via:

- His website: www.simonjackson.co.uk

- LinkedIn: www.linkedin.com/in/simonjacksoncoach

- Bluesky: @simonjackson.co.uk

Acknowledgements

It was April 2012, and my wife Sara and I were in our favourite restaurant in Manchester, celebrating her birthday. As we sat back with a cocktail at the end of the meal, I told her there was something I needed to talk about. 'I'm thinking of leaving Vodafone and setting up my own coaching business.' Before I could run through all the points I'd prepared – the business case, the risks, the financials, the fact that we had three children under the age of six, a sizeable mortgage, and absolutely no experience of running my own company – Sara just smiled and said, 'Do it. You'll love it. You'll be great.' With those eight words, she gave me her unconditional support. And with that kind of belief behind me, how could I possibly fail?

That was the beginning. And everything that followed – including this book – had Sara's support running through it. For that, I was eternally grateful.

There's another person whose support has spanned this entire journey: Lynn Pickford. Coach, mentor, confidante, butt-kicker, occasional therapist, and above all, friend. Lynn has seen the doubts, the false starts, the rewrites – and she never flinched. She's asked the right questions at the right time, challenged me when I needed it, and held space when I didn't know quite what I was trying to say. She's been the person in the room every author needs but rarely finds. I wouldn't have got to the end of this project without her.

It's customary – but nonetheless richly deserved – to thank my publisher, Alison Jones, and the team at Practical Inspiration Publishing, for helping make this book real. From the first conversation to the final proof, Alison has brought encouragement, challenge, and structure in exactly the right measure. Kelly Winter, the project manager at Newgen Publishing UK, has been a calm and reassuring presence behind the scenes, guiding the production process with professionalism and patience. And Ginny Carter, whose guidance during the writing phase helped shape the direction of the book, also deserves my sincere thanks.

Thank you to Paul Dodd, the 'Ideas Man' behind ALLGOOD, whose illustrations added both clarity and character to the final book. It's a pleasure when someone brings your ideas to life better than you imagined them.

I also want to acknowledge Damian Hughes, who kindly wrote the Foreword. Damian has played a bigger part in my journey than he probably realizes. His thinking, generosity, and example have all influenced the path I've taken – and I'm grateful to have his voice help introduce this work.

There are, of course, far too many people to name. But to all those who've walked alongside me in some way – thank you. To friends, colleagues, and fellow travellers who've offered ideas, feedback, encouragement, or simply shown up at the right moment: I see you and I'm grateful.

And finally, to my clients. The people I work with every day are the reason I get to keep learning, thinking, improving. Thank you for the trust you place in me, and for the opportunity to grow alongside you.

Writing a book is an act of creation, but it's rarely a solo effort. Like most meaningful things, it's built on relationships. This book may have my name on the cover, but it has many fingerprints on its pages.

Appendix

List of core values

Abundance	Acceptance	Accomplishment	Accountability	Accuracy	Achievement
Acknowledgement	Adaptability	Advancement	Adventure	Affection	Agility
Alertness	Altruism	Ambition	Amusement	Anticipation	Appreciation
Assertiveness	Attentiveness	Authority	Awareness	Balance	Beauty
Being the best	Belonging	Blissfulness	Boldness	Bravery	Brilliance
Calm	Candour	Capability	Carefulness	Caring	Caution
Certainty	Challenge	Change	Charity	Cheerfulness	Cleanliness
Collaboration	Comfort	Commitment	Common sense	Communication	Community
Compassion	Competence	Competitiveness	Concentration	Conciseness	Confidence
Connection	Consciousness	Consistency	Contentment	Continuity	Contribution
Control	Conviction	Cooperation	Courage	Courtesy	Creativity
Credibility	Curiosity	Daring	Decisiveness	Dedication	Delight
Democracy	Dependability	Desire	Determination	Development	Devotion
Dignity	Diligence	Discipline	Discovery	Discretion	Diversity
Drive	Duty	Eagerness	Education	Effectiveness	Efficiency
Elation	Elegance	Empathy	Empower	Encouragement	Endurance
Energy	Enjoyment	Enthusiasm	Entrepreneurship	Equality	Ethical
Excellence	Excitement	Experience	Expertise	Exploration	Expressiveness
Fairness	Faith	Fame	Family	Fearless	Feelings
Ferocious	Fidelity	Financial security	Flexibility	Flow	Focus
Foresight	Forgiveness	Fortitude	Freedom	Friendship	Frugality
Fun	Generosity	Genius	Giving	Goodness	Grace
Gratitude	Greatness	Growth	Guidance	Happiness	Hard work
Harmony	Health	Helpfulness	Heroism	Holiness	Honesty

Honour	Hopefulness	Hospitality	Humility	Humour	Imagination
Impact	Improvement	Independence	Individuality	Influence	Ingenuity
Initiative	Inner peace	Innovation	Inquisitive	Insightfulness	Inspiration
Integrity	Intelligence	Intensity	Intimacy	Intuitiveness	Inventiveness
Involvement	Joy	Justice	Kindness	Knowledge	Lawful
Leadership	Learning	Legacy	Liberty	Logic	Longevity
Love	Loyalty	Making a difference	Mastery	Maturity	Meaning
Merit	Mindfulness	Moderation	Modesty	Money	Motivation
Nature	Openness	Opportunity	Optimism	Order	Organization
Orientation	Originality	Outcome	Outstanding	Passion	Patience
Peace	Perceptiveness	Performance	Perseverance	Persistence	Personal growth
Physicality	Playfulness	Pleasure	Poise	Positive attitude	Potential
Power	Practicality	Precision	Preparedness	Presence	Preservation
Prestige	Privacy	Proactivity	Productivity	Professionalism	Progress
Prosperity	Public service	Punctuality	Purpose	Quality	Quiet
Rationality	Realistic	Reason	Recognition	Recreation	Reflective
Relationships	Reliability	Religion	Resourcefulness	Respect	Responsibility
Restraint	Results-oriented	Reverence	Righteousness	Rigour	Risk-taking
Romance	Safety	Satisfaction	Security	Self-esteem	Self-reliance
Selflessness	Sensitivity	Serenity	Seriousness	Service	Sharing
Significance	Silence	Simplicity	Sincerity	Skilfulness	Smart
Socialising	Solitude	Speed	Spirit	Spirituality	Spontaneous
Stability	Status	Stewardship	Strength	Structure	Style
Success	Support	Surprise	Sustainability	Systemisation	Talent
Teamwork	Temperance	Thankful	Thorough	Thoughtful	Timeliness
Tolerance	Toughness	Tradition	Tranquillity	Transparency	Trust
Trustworthy	Truth	Understanding	Uniqueness	Unity	Valour
Variety	Victory	Vigour	Vision	Vitality	Wealth
Welcoming	Well-being	Winning	Wisdom	Wonder	

Index

www.ingramcontent.com/pod-product-compliance
Lightning Source LLC
Chambersburg PA
CBHW022102210326
41518CB00039B/385